What Was There for Me Once

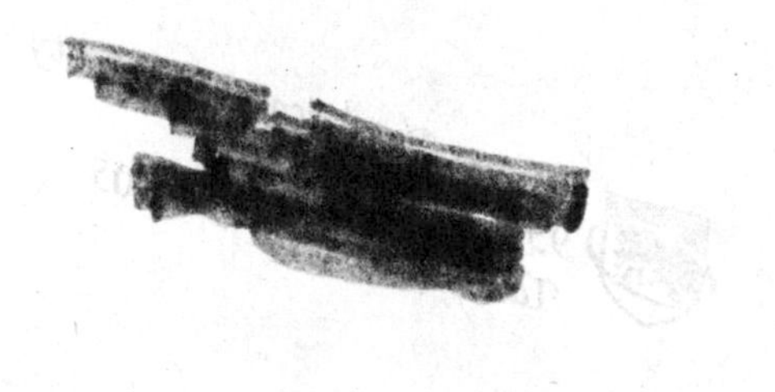

What Was There for Me Once

A Memoir

Margaret R. Brennan, IHM

NOVALIS

Cover design: Blair Turner
Cover and interior images: courtesy of Margaret Brennan
Layout: Audrey Wells

Business Offices:
Novalis Publishing Inc.
10 Lower Spadina Avenue, Suite 400
Toronto, Ontario, Canada
M5V 2Z2

Novalis Publishing Inc.
4475 Frontenac Street
Montréal, Québec
Canada H2H 2S2

Phone: 1-800-387-7164
Fax: 1-800-204-4140
E-mail: books@novalis.ca

www.novalis.ca

Library and Archives Canada Cataloguing in Publication

Brennan, Margaret R., 1924–
What was there for me once : a memoir / Margaret R. Brennan.

ISBN 978-2-89646-127-1

1. Brennan, Margaret R., 1924-. 2. Nuns--Michigan--Monroe--Biography.
3. Sisters, Servants of the Immaculate Heart of Mary--Biography.
4. Feminist spirituality. I. Title.

BX4705.B8356 A3 2009 271'.903 C2009-900950-1

Printed in Canada.

We acknowledge the financial support of the Government of Canada through the Book Publishing Industry Development Program (BPIDP) for our publishing activities.

5 4 3 2 1 13 12 11 10 09

Contents

Dedication

To Kilian McDonnell, OSB,
who was the first "prompter" of this memoir

and to Mary Jo Leddy,
who saw it through to the finish.

Old paint on canvas, as it ages, sometimes becomes transparent. When that happens it is possible, in some pictures, to see the original lines: a tree will show through a woman's dress, a child makes way for a dog, a large boat is no longer on an open sea. That is called pentimento because the painter "repented," changed his mind. Perhaps it would be as well to say that the old conception, replaced by a later choice, is a way of seeing and then seeing again.

... The paint has aged now and I wanted to see what was there for me once, what is there for me now.

—Lillian Hellman, *Pentimento*

Introduction

Over the course of my life, I have seen at least three major repaintings of religious life. At times, I have been one of the painters, although certainly not the only one. My most active and obvious participation in this process was from 1966 to 1976.

However, this was not only a process I helped to shape; it was also a process that shaped me. In this sense, I have become a living canvas holding many images of religious life.

A number of people have encouraged me to write my memoirs—to tell my part of the story of what happened to religious life in the United States during a crucial period of history. This has been a welcome opportunity for me to think about a process I was so involved in but rarely had time to assess. It is only now that the meaning of the events and developments I participated in is becoming more transparent to me. I wrote this book out of the desire to see what was there for me once and what is there for me now.

In the first chapter, I describe my roots—my family, my faith and my city. Then, I evoke the memory of the traditional religious life I entered and loved. Although it remained largely unaltered for centuries, it changed almost overnight and then again … and again. The central two parts of the book detail the changes to religious life after the epoch-making experience of the Second Vatican Council. At the time, I was involved in the leadership of my own community (the Sister Servants of the Immaculate Heart of Mary in Monroe, Michigan) and in the newly formed Leadership Conference of Women Religious. It was during this period that I saw up close the repainting of religious life, for better or for worse. The final chapter outlines what is there for me now in religious life.

This book is neither an autobiography nor a detailed history of religious life in the United States. It is a collection of memories, partial but true. Memories serve us well when they present us with the possibility of making choices and making promises that will make a difference in the future.

My story bears little resemblance to those narratives that recall great and glorious sweeps of history or describe the pathos of the tides of suffering that usually exist somewhere in our world. But in my own limited way, I would like to bear witness to the journey of women in the United States with whom I walked during an unrepeatable period in the history of the Catholic Church.

I

The Original Lines

1

Growing Up Catholic and American

I was born into an Irish-American family in which the traditional faith was vibrant and strong. My father, Henry Brennan, was a contractor who built many of the Catholic institutions in the Detroit area: the mother houses of the Immaculate Heart of Mary (IHM) Sisters, the provincial house of the Felician Sisters, the friary of the Franciscans, the Carmelite and Dominican monasteries, and the Sacred Heart and St. John provincial seminaries. Our family was built on the Church, but my father also, quite literally, built the church in Detroit.

The W. E. Wood company, of which my father became president at an early age, was well known in the city. It built churches and educational institutions as well as auto manufacturing plants and office buildings. My father had a fine architectural sense and would often criticize the plans he had to follow. I recall one instance when he was given the contract to build a church that reflected the sharp lines and brassy aspects of modern design. "Do not put the company sign on that construction site," he ordered. "It looks like a goddamn theatre!"

Henry J. Brennan was a man who had a well-developed sense of values and high moral standards. However, we rarely heard them articulated, except through my mother. My father, I sensed, expected her to tell us how he felt about many aspects of life. My mother, Ann Elizabeth Markey, had been a teacher before she married my father. Her even temperament and wise powers of discernment were a perfect balance for his volatile and aggressive sides. In every sense, she was the "hearth" of our home. I suspect that some feminists would criticize some of her handling of my father. I recall that one or another of us had to stand guard near the kitchen and warn her of my father's approach when she was frying the steak that he insisted be broiled. She would deftly place it under the broiler at the last minute and would smile when he later noted with satisfaction that "there was nothing like a broiled steak"!

Nevertheless, my mother was very much her own person. On one occasion, my brother Henry was home on leave from the navy during the Second World War. He was to have met my father at the office but did not arrive at the expected time. Impatient and put out, my father called home. He inquired loudly and impatiently, "Where the hell is he?" My mother quietly hung up the phone. "Your father should not speak that way from the office," she said. That evening he came home with flowers for her—but not a word of apology, at least not that those of us around heard tell.

Both my parents had a high regard for education. Unlike many men of the time, my father expected that the girls as well as the boys would go to college. All four of us girls attended Marygrove College in Detroit, while the boys attended the University of Detroit, sponsored by the Jesuits. Marygrove, a liberal arts college for women which had an excellent reputation, was owned and sponsored by the IHM Sisters from Monroe, Michigan. My father's mostly unarticulated attitude of equality for women comes through clearly on my mother's tombstone in the Brennan plot at Holy Sepulchre cemetery in Detroit. It simply reads, "Ann Elizabeth Markey, wife of Henry J. Brennan." He insisted that her maiden name was important, even in death.

Thinking back, however, I sense now that my parents came from families that regarded education as highly for women as for men. Julia Brennan, my father's sister, was one of the first female lawyers in Detroit. Sister Marianna Markey, IHM, my mother's sister, was a fine educator who authored a series of elementary school readers.

The Catholic faith was part of the fabric of our family's daily life. It did not seem to be something special; rather, it was just a part of growing up. We often had priests over for meals; we children thought it was normal to have "Father" at the table with us. My father and mother each had a brother who was a priest and a sister who was a religious. Sister Ann Vincent Brennan, IHM, was the administrator of The Hall of the Divine Child in Monroe for most of her IHM life. (The Hall, commonly known as HDC, was a boys' boarding school for grades 1 to 8.) Sister Marianna Markey, IHM, was both an author and an educator, particularly of elementary school children. These two "sister aunts" did not figure so prominently in our growing-up years because IHM sisters of that time were not allowed to visit their home; family visits, which were always to the convent, were restricted to a very few times a year. My mother's brother Harold J. Markey was a diocesan priest who taught at the local Sacred Heart Seminary for a time, and later became pastor of two large city parishes. He was in many ways larger than life. A great promoter of the Catholic Youth Organization, he was deeply committed to the summer camps that gave young boys from the city an experience of nature. He also did chaplaincy work at the city jails, especially with young people. He was my mother's youngest brother, and I sensed they were very close to one another. He came for dinner most Sunday nights. My mother's death was a keen loss for him, and he remained very close to my father afterwards.

Vincent L. Brennan, my father's priest brother, was a Jesuit. We were told when growing up that Father Vince had always wanted to go to the missions, but that Grandma (who was a great one for prayer) had managed to "arrange" for this not to happen. He spent most of his priestly life teaching theology in Chicago but, in later years, was stationed at the University of Detroit, which brought him closer to us. Father Vince had a fine sense of humour, though he was a little more committed to the letter of the law than was Father Harold. Perhaps that was because Father Vince taught moral theology, which had little "give" in the pre-Vatican Church. His brother Jesuits called him "Mike," for what reason I do not know. After he retired from formal teaching, he remained in the Jesuit residence at the university and on Sundays would often help out in parishes. One Sunday, on his way home, he stopped at a drugstore in a dangerous and depressed neighbourhood. As he got out of the car, a young man pressed a pistol into his back, saying, "Gimme your money, Padre."

Without blinking, he replied, "Go to hell!" The young man, more startled by such a reply than Father Vince was by the would-be robber with the gun, took off on the double! On arriving back at the Jesuit residence, Father Vince related the incident to his confreres. "Mike," said one, "he could have shot you."

"Never before noon," was Mike's reply.

While each of us seven Brennan siblings had his or her friends and pastimes, family meals together—especially dinner in the evening—were an expected part of everyday life. At the dinner table, each of us had a place, and we never deviated from it. Every Sunday, we went to Mass as a family and then returned home for a big breakfast together. Often on Sunday mornings or afternoons, my father and mother would go to visit their own mothers and take two or three of us along. At Grandma Markey's we had tea and sugar cookies, while at Grandma Brennan's we were treated to port wine and fruitcake.

It would be true to say that our family was financially comfortable, and we didn't grow up worrying too much about the necessities of life. However, my older brothers and sisters tell of some major shifts in lifestyle during the Great Depression, about which I have little or no recollection. We, like many other families, had our own traditions. On Christmas morning, for example, we would all line up "in rank" at the top of the stairs and go down together to find our gifts. Mine were always on the centre section of the leather couch in the library where our Christmas tree stood in all its glorious array. It never entered my mind to question why the tree was in the library and not in the living room, but one of my older sisters later told me. It seemed that after Grandma Brennan's eldest son, Richard, died as a very young man, she would never have a Christmas tree in her house and always dressed in black. I am not sure what this must have meant to her eight younger children. Yet, out of respect for his mother, who always came to Christmas dinner at our house, my father put our tree in the library.

Our home had an air of hospitality about it, and we were happy to make room for others. My six sisters and brothers would bring friends home for meals, during which there was always stimulating conversation and good-natured badgering. Birthdays were special events to which my Grandma Brennan was always invited, and she baked whatever kind of cake we wanted. Our summers were spent at a summer home on Lake Huron, where lots of friends would join us for weekends.

After my Uncle Ed died, sometime in my early teens, Uncle Ray, my mother's bachelor brother, came to live with us. He had lived with Uncle Ed and Grandma Markey for many years. Even now I can touch the sadness I felt that first evening at dinner. Uncle Ray, sitting across the table from me and next to my mother, kept fighting back what seemed like an ocean of tears that kept welling up in his eyes. It was the first time I had seen a man cry. Uncle Ray's left side had been paralyzed when a severe virus had gotten out of control and affected several young men at Camp Custer, where he was stationed during the First World War. As a result, he always walked with cane and could not drive a car. He worked at the traffic office in downtown Detroit, walking a block each morning to catch the bus. Many friends of my brothers knew him as Uncle Ray and would come to him with their parking tickets, hoping that he could intervene for them. In the summers at Port Huron, after he had retired from the traffic office, he would open his "store" on the front lawn in the afternoons, and we could choose from a large number and variety of candy bars that he kept in his room. The neighbours were included as well. It was a sweet time for us all.

Looking back on my life at home, I can say that we all had a deep feeling for one another but that we rarely, if ever, articulated it. And so it was that on the July morning in 1945 when I left home for the mother house of the IHM Sisters in Monroe, my mother and father and I acted as if we could have been going anywhere. What we all felt went unsaid that day, but flowed so deeply that I can still touch it, even now, as I write this some 60 years later. At that time, I was 21 and had graduated from college just a few weeks before. I was extroverted and fun-loving, and my decision to enter religious life was a shock to my friends and family alike. My "little brother" Marty (then about 15) was the only boy at home, since the other two were still at war. When I told him about my decision to "go to Monroe" (which meant "the convent"), he responded solemnly. Not knowing what else to say, I suppose, he said, "Well, Marg, as Jesus said, 'What does it profit a man if he gain the whole world and suffer the loss of his soul?'"

I laughed at the time, wondering whether he thought that I was in grave spiritual danger of some kind. I later discovered that this scripture passage was a stock phrase for him (learned from the Jesuits he so revered). He quoted it to his seven children on various and sundry occasions. It was no surprise that, when I went to his funeral in 2006, this text of St. Mark would be on the memorial card marking his death, along with the initials AMDG (*ad majorem Dei gloriam*, the motto of the Jesuits, which means "for the greater glory of God").

There is nothing dramatic in the story of my vocation to religious life. There was no sudden illumination, nor was my decision accompanied by a long and difficult discernment.

Along with my three sisters (Mary Catherine, Ann and Ellen), I attended the Academy of the Sacred Heart, a day school run by the Religious of the Sacred Heart. There, we received a superb education in the liberal arts tradition. Because the school was small, we had opportunities as students to establish close relationships with the nuns and with one another. We were, in many ways, part of the religious family of the Sacred Heart. Feast days and holy days, solemn processions and special occasions when we wore our white uniforms marked the passage of the year. The spiritual life of the students grew and developed not only through religion classes and the general atmosphere of the school, but most especially by our entrance into each of the four sodalities that marked our passage and growth in what I would call "wisdom, age and grace." Each sodality had its own distinguishing medal, special name, practices and forms of prayer, as well as a commitment to service of others. The culmination of this spiritual journey was entrance into the Children of Mary sodality, which occurred in senior year. The ceremony during which we received the Child of Mary sodality medal was a solemn occasion and ritual. Those who received the medal formed a relationship with the Society of the Sacred Heart that is deep and enduring, linking the recipient with Sacred Heart alumnae around the world.

During my twelve years at Lawrence Avenue (Sacred Heart schools were frequently named after the streets or sometimes the neighbourhoods in which they were located), I do not recall ever hearing a vocation talk and did not think much about such a call. However, near the end of my sophomore or junior year, I distinctly remember dealing with a vocational "intrusion," coming from I know not where.

Until then, I had been certain that I did not want to be a nun. My decision seemed definite to me. Nevertheless, the fear that I might "want to want to" began to make an inroad into my mind. In retrospect, it seems providential that none of the nuns ever broached the topic with me. The sense of vocation seemed to have emerged from deep within me. In the fall of 1941, after my graduation from Lawrence Avenue in June, I entered Marygrove College, and the small invitational voice receded into the background for several years.

As I ponder the mystery of my own vocation, I would say that it grew and developed at Marygrove. Perhaps I was more ready to give a hearing to the unwanted invitation I had received in high school. My college years began and ended with our country's participation in the Second World War. The war shaped the kind of college education I received. In addition to a rigorous scholastic program, each student was also expected to take on some form of social action. Inspiring speakers, including Dorothy Day and the Baroness Catherine de Hueck, addressed us on the social questions of the day, challenging us as women to use our power to make a difference.

As I look back on those college days, I marvel that the sisters brought two such strong and outspoken women in to speak to us. They shocked us! Dorothy Day – social activist and co-founder of the Catholic Worker movement in 1933, which promoted nonviolence and hospitality for the poor – walked down the main aisle of the auditorium in a baggy tweed suit smoking a cigarette, followed by Sister Honora, the very dignified president of the college. In her address, Day encouraged us in those years of the war to try to convince our brothers, friends and fiancés to be conscientious objectors, even if they were already in the armed forces. Her message did not go over well, since hardly a young woman in the college was not affected by that war. We regularly sang such rousing songs as "Remember Pearl Harbor As We Go to Meet the Foe" and "Praise the Lord and Pass the Ammunition." It was a time of high patriotism, and we were not prepared for Day's strong commitment to non-violence, even though many students did ministry in settlement houses in the city, inspired by Dorothy Day.

Catherine de Hueck, a former member of the Russian nobility, had immigrated to Canada in 1921. Now a social activist, she founded the Madonna House Apostolate and worked tirelessly for the poor. She addressed the sisters (who sat in the balcony) rather than the students, challenging the sisters to get "out of your pink-tiled bathrooms" and be out with the poor! A group of nuns in New York was less than welcoming to her. (I was sure that IHM sisters did not have pink-tiled bathrooms, and the evidence bore out this suspicion in the years to come.)

It was only in my junior year that I once again gave the "want to want to" voice a hearing. The IHM sisters who taught me had stimulated a slumbering desire in me; moreover, they were not reticent about asking the questions that unlocked what had lain deep within me.

By the fall of 1944, I was sure of my direction, although I was not yet certain of exactly where I wanted to go. For a short time I thought about joining the Carmelites, who had a monastery on the property of the college. I had already begun to read St. Teresa of Avila, St. Thérèse of the Child Jesus (the Little Flower), and the works of Dom Marmion, OSB. Yet, I was also attracted to Maryknoll and a life in the missions. In the end, it seemed that the IHM congregation combined both of these desires. In some sense, the IHMs were also in my genes, since my father and mother each had a sister in the order. A few weeks before entering the IHM community, I returned to the Academy on Lawrence Avenue to tell the nuns of my decision. When they asked, "Why aren't you coming to us?" I could only reply, "Nobody ever asked me."

2

A More Perfect Way

As I unpacked my suitcase in the postulate at Monroe on that Sunday night, July 1, 1945, I saw that my father and mother had pinned letters to my robe. I knew by instinct that if I opened them that night, I would not be able to deal with the depth of feelings that would flood over me, and I might not have the strength to stay. Later, I gave them unopened to a professed sister who was a friend, asking her to keep them for me. It was 25 years later when I asked at last to have them back and read them. This reveals something about myself that I cannot completely fathom, even now. In the letters, my mother and father—each in their own way—wrote of their deep love for me, their desire for my happiness, and what my personality and presence had meant to them. They both assured me that if I discovered that religious life was not for me, I would be welcomed home with open arms.

The war ended shortly after I entered the convent, although we did not know any of the details about how the end of the war happened. We neither looked at television (which was a new phenomenon) nor listened to the radio. Moreover, on that August evening in 1945, we were still in the midst of our annual retreat, which was conducted in solemn silence. When I first heard the wonderful news that the war was over, I expected that we would all come out of retreat and celebrate. Instead, we had an extra holy hour of prayer in thanksgiving. Later, back in the area of the mother house where the postulants lived, I found myself looking out the window from the third floor. It was early evening and the western sky was still streaked with brilliant red, yellow and orange from the setting sun. I can still recall a feeling of great joy mixed with deep loneliness. My mind took flight to Port Huron and our home on the lake. I pictured my parents, sisters and youngest brother celebrating the end of the war with friends and neighbours. My brothers and brother-in-law, my sister's fiancé and many friends would finally be returning home after months and years away, most of them having been stationed in the South Pacific. These images filled my mind, and I felt a sharp pain in my heart, a longing to be with my family.

The six months in the postulate were difficult for me. I could not relate to the youthful enthusiasm of most of my 52 companions, the majority of whom had entered the convent just out of high school. And I was deeply lonesome. As visiting Sunday approached, I looked forward with both joy and anguish to seeing my family, knowing that when the visit ended, it would be another three months before I saw them again.

One Sunday near the end of my postulate, my mother brought me several new sets of underwear in her big purse. "Take these upstairs and exchange them for the old ones." I insisted that I had no need of them, since all I had to do was ask for new ones from the postulant mistress. Nevertheless, my mother was adamant, because she had a clear memory of her own mother many years before saving bleached flour sacks for the nuns at St. Vincent Convent in Detroit. "They make underwear from them," her mother had said. Clearly, my mother had no intention of my wearing flour-sack underwear.

"Motherrrrrr! That was a long time ago," I replied. Imagine my shock on the very first night after I received the habit and moved to the novitiate wing of the building: there in front of me, jauntily walking down the dormitory corridor, was Sister Alberta, a young second-year novice. Her nightcap leaned rakishly to the left on her shorn head and her black ankle-length cotton skirt served as a housecoat covering her nightgown, on the back of which were the faded but still legible words "fifty pounds chicken feed." I never mentioned this discovery to my mother.

Entrance into the novitiate took place on a wintry day in January. The ceremony was a solemn one, with many priests in attendance, and was presided over by Cardinal Edward Mooney, our local archbishop. Our families filled the chapel. In some ways, this was a time of sadness for them—their relationship with us was about to change.

Together with my many classmates, I processed down the middle aisle in a white satin dress and white bridal veil. The dresses were kept in a big cedar closet and used year after year, with adjustments made to them as needed. A large carton contained white shoes of various styles and sizes. Most of us were able to find a suitable pair—quite an accomplishment given that there were over 50 of us in the class.

The Cardinal told our parents that even though what was about to happen was, in a sense, a break with the world, in time, they would find that the bonds we had with our families would be deeper than ever.

Many, many years later, at my golden jubilee celebration, my eldest brother, Richard, recalled those words in his toast. I was touched that he remembered them—and I hoped that my family had found them to be true.

To symbolize that we were leaving the world and a former existence, the Cardinal cut off a lock of our hair. We left the chapel through doors near the sanctuary. Professed sisters helped us as we were robed in the habit and white veil of the novices. I can still recall—and feel, a bit—the initial shock when one of the professed sisters wrapped a towel around my shoulders, gently bent my head forward, and very efficiently removed all of my hair with an electric razor. All this was done with great precision, as there were 50 young postulants that afternoon who had to be clothed in the habit and veil. Because my hair was a mousey brown and straight as a stick, it had no particular attraction for Sister Josetta, who made beautiful wigs of real hair for the dolls sold in the gift shop. I noted, even amid my shock at being "shorn," how deftly she scooped up the beautiful red and blond hair of two of my companions! At the time, most of us were too excited by the drama of it all to take in what had just happened. Indeed, we had lost our hair ... all of it! Accompanied by a hymn to St. Alphonsus Liguori (the patron of the congregation) and the sonorous tones of the organ, we processed back up the long aisle again. It was a dramatic change; I could hear some muffled sobs as we walked past our families. The Cardinal announced our new names, symbolizing once more our new reality. Henceforth, I was to be known as Sister Benedicta.

My two priest uncles were in attendance. Both had a word of wisdom to offer me later, when I visited with my family in the parlour.

"Now, Benedicta," said Monsignor Markey, my mother's brother, "don't get too scrupulous with that rule. Sit the saddle with ease!" Father Brennan, my father's Jesuit brother, offered more solemn advice, although with a playful tone: "The rule is a road to holiness. Jump out of that bed in the morning as though it were on fire!"

Surprisingly, perhaps, entering the novitiate was for me like being Alice in Wonderland. My whole world turned around. Everything seemed new and beautiful, and the world as I had known it faded away. I quickly adapted to the monastic structure, the silence, the unchanging order of the day. Life in the novitiate followed a very regular pattern. We rose every day at 5:00 a.m. and were in bed by 9:30 p.m. The bell would ring before every exercise of the day, which would start with a prayer, and thus every hour of the day was sanctified.

We slept in dormitories of six, nine or twelve novices. After rising (with the first sound of the bell!), we would have half an hour of meditation followed by Mass. This was followed by a simple breakfast in silence, accompanied by a reading from *The Imitation of Christ* by Thomas à Kempis. We took all our meals in silence except for those on Thursday evening, Sunday afternoon, and all day Saturday. At our meals we listened to readings from the lives of the saints or some other spiritual book.

There were periods of recreation twice a day, the first after lunch and the second after supper. During those times, we were allowed to talk, and I remember plenty of laughter bursting forth. We learned how to entertain each other with very few things. If the weather was good, we went for a walk. Sometimes it seemed to me that we looked like a flock of geese following the gander! Often we visited the community cemetery. The novice mistress would tell us stories about various sisters who had gone before us. In the winter, we skated on the pond behind the mother house, and in the warmer months played many games of baseball. I have memories of quiet, beautiful summer evenings when, after we had been picking beans and berries, the night prayer bell rang. We walked home in silence like contemplative Trappist monks returning from the fields. Every Sunday morning, we were in retreat until the noon meal; on the first Sunday of the month, we had a full-day retreat. Holy Week was also a very solemn time of silence, and each summer we made a retreat of eight full days.

In the mornings, we attended classes on religious life with the novice mistress. We also had our "charges": serving meals, working in the infirmary, and cleaning the immense mother house. Life became very predictable and was ordered according to transcendent values. This routine enabled us to focus on the changing liturgical seasons that gave colour to our lives. We learned to sing the contemplative beauty of Gregorian chant as well as majestic choral pieces. The purple of Advent and the rose-coloured vestments on Gaudete Sunday, the drama of Holy

Week with the singing of Tenebrae, the splendour of Easter and the fiery tongues of Pentecost—all these had a profound effect on the way we imagined our lives within a longer and deeper narrative of meaning.

On Christmas morning, a few minutes before the usual rising bell, we put on our starched white linen veils and sang carols as we carried a statue of the Infant Jesus to the postulants and to the door of each professed sister before the common meditation period. The Christmas liturgy was solemn and joyful at the same time. Because it was such a special feast, we could talk during the whole day, visit with the professed sisters and partake of the candy, nuts and fruits that seemed to be everywhere throughout the convent.

The first year of the novitiate was the "canonical" year. During this time we were to have no outside distractions or formal classes. The time was to be devoted entirely to spiritual formation and to learning how to be an IHM sister. We were also introduced to the spiritual life and learned a method of mental prayer. Each day we had morning meditation, said the rosary, made the Stations of the Cross, did spiritual reading and made a fifteen-minute visit to the Blessed Sacrament. Our devotions reflected the spirituality of St. Alphonsus Liguori, since our congregation had been founded by Louis Gillet, a Redemptorist missionary in Monroe, and Theresa Duchemin, a former Oblate Sister of Providence from Baltimore. Both were imbued with the spirituality of St. Alphonsus Liguori, with its emphasis on the liberating mission of Jesus, especially to the poor and abandoned. The required reading in the novitiate was the three volumes of *Christian Perfection* by Alphonsus Rodriguez, SJ. Finding them tedious and boring, filled with heroic exploits of the desert fathers and their sayings, I raced through them as fast as I could. At last, the novice mistress gave me other books on prayer, and I began my initial but serious reading of St. Teresa of Avila, a patroness of our congregation: St. Alphonsus, a doctor of prayer, said he had learned to pray from her. Gradually, I was being introduced to the great and wise teachers of the spiritual life.

During this time I definitely withdrew from the world as I had known it and entered into another. This was an unusual act for me, since I had been very interested, especially during the war, in what was going on around me. I had followed the progress of the war intently, and paid careful attention to the subtle and not so subtle changes that resulted from more women entering the workforce. In the novitiate, we knew next to nothing of what was happening "out there." I never saw or read a newspaper, and those of us who worked in the infirmary were cautioned against reading any of the newspapers that were used to wrap leftovers from the trays.

The novitiate was a very ordered, centred and, for me, joyful way of life. We were being formed in a monastic, semi-cloistered lifestyle even though we were members of an apostolic congregation. Later, I would learn that this was true of most congregations of women religious in the United States

During our two years in the novitiate, we learned about living in community. This meant that everyone had the same things and lived in the same way. Thus, we had a very simple lifestyle. We had a good habit, to be worn only on special occasions, and a regular habit for the rest of the time. We were allowed neither fountain pens nor watches.

Entrance into the novitiate with a new name was symbolic of a new way of life and of becoming a new person. In our novitiate instruction classes, we learned about the three vows that all religious took: poverty, chastity and obedience. Poverty meant having really nothing of your own except what was provided for your use. What we learned about chastity was to strive to love God alone. This implied that we were to avoid particular friendships so as to have this singular love. Our instructions were to love everybody equally. This focus on loving God placed our human lives in perspective: we were allowed visits from our family four times a year and wrote home every month, but we neither wrote nor received letters during Lent. When Easter came during my first year in the novitiate, a long rectangular box arrived, addressed to me in my mother's inimitable Palmer Method handwriting. The novice mistress gave the parcel to me to open. Inside was a scroll tied with bright yellow ribbon. It contained 40 pages glued together—one for each day of Lent. The introductory page read "Forty Days at Brennans." Each page related some interesting or very simple reflection or anecdote of what was happening at home. Often there were references to letters from my brothers overseas, and concerns and fretting when my sister Ann did not get a letter from Bill, her fiancé-to-be. Sometimes my mother would paste his letter in the window of the front door so that my sister would see it on her way up the steps as she arrived home from work. My mother described everyday events of the week, and often referred to Sunday nights, when Father Harold would stop in for a supper of Welsh rarebit (cheese on toast). And always she would end with the reminder to remember her at "angel's time" (evening Angelus), when she would be thinking of me.

God's will, as we learned in the novitiate, was static and unchanging. God had a plan: a blueprint for the Church and for the lives of each of us. Our task was to discover that will, which we perceived to be somehow outside of us. We were never asked to *think* about God's will for us. We *knew* what God's will was because we had a rule of life that had been approved by the appropriate channels in Rome— a sort of a Good Housekeeping Seal of Approval. Obedience to God was made tangible by the perfect keeping of that rule. "Keep the Rule and the Rule will keep you" was an adage that we all knew and tried to internalize. Keeping that rule perfectly was often called a kind of martyrdom, which in some sense it was.

The Church governed our lives through the Sacred Congregation for Religious, the office in the Vatican to which all religious congregations were responsible. It was the Sacred Congregation in Rome that approved our rule and any changes that we might wish to make to it. This rule guided our way of life down to the minutest detail. Any major deviation from its observance or change required specific permission from Roman authorities. This requirement was so all-inclusive that even the superiors did not have the right to change the order of the day. We prided ourselves on such attention from the Vatican, believing it to mean that we were a special class of persons, as indeed we were: we were endeavouring to enter what St. Thomas Aquinas had called (and the Church had endorsed) "the state of perfection"—a way of life and being towards which we were to strive, even though it was unattainable. Moreover, it was a sure guarantee that if we kept the rule perfectly we would become saints—something to which we all aspired. There was something immensely heroic about such idealism. As a way of life, it also had the potential to generate greatness or pettiness of spirit.

Life in the novitiate was not happy for everyone, but it was for me. I have wondered whether this was because I entered religious life after college, older and more experienced, and so was able to keep focused on the heart of the matter. I sensed that those of us who came to religious life in our early 20s had a better sense of who we were as persons than those who were seventeen or eighteen. Some of the younger novices seemed to lose their identities; it would be a long struggle for some of them to find themselves as the years passed.

In November of my first year of the novitiate, my sister Ann was married. Of course, I was not allowed to attend, because religious did not go to weddings. I remember the day very well. As I folded sheets in the laundry, I tried to picture everything about the ceremony. The wedding had a sad tinge to it, since my sister was marrying a non-Catholic. In the pre-Vatican Church, such marriages were highly discouraged. My sister could not have a church wedding in the normal sense of the word. No liturgy marked this joyous occasion. Instead, the engaged couple stood outside of the sanctuary before the altar of the Blessed Mother to make their vows, but received no nuptial blessing.

Moreover, the non-Catholic partner had to promise to raise all the children Catholic.

Thankfully, many significant changes have occurred in interchurch and interfaith marriages since the Second Vatican Council. Today, with the permission of the bishop, the marriage ceremony can even take place following the rite of the non-Catholic's religious tradition. In November 2006, my sister and her husband, whose marriage the Church tolerated but would not bless, celebrated 60 years of life together in the company of their children, grandchildren and great-grandchildren.

Some years ago, Ann's husband, Bill, entered the Church. He had accompanied his family to Mass for many, many years, had attended the Catholic baptisms and weddings of his children and grandchildren, and had been present at numerous events in the Catholic schools they attended. For Bill, there was no need for faith instruction. He said it best himself: "I am not a convert. I have simply become who I am."

Priests and bishops would come to the IHM mother house regularly; and of course they were even closer to God than we were. After all, bishops weren't just *striving* for perfection. They were, according to St. Thomas Aquinas, *in* the state of perfection! The esteem we held for the priesthood was above and beyond our regard for anything else. As it happened, the year I entered the novitiate was the 100th anniversary of the IHM congregation. That summer there was an immense celebration, and I saw several hundred priests, monsignori and bishops arrive to celebrate the Mass of Thanksgiving at the mother house. A special centennial chalice had been crafted and adorned with precious stones and gold taken from rings and other jewellery that had belonged to sisters before entering or had been given as gifts by members of their families.

After the Mass, all the clergy were invited to an elaborate banquet that included fine wine and cigars. Some of the young professed sisters were chosen to serve and felt honoured to do so. Elaborate and eloquent speeches, given for the most part by bishops, lauded both the history and ministry of the congregation. The sisters listened from loudspeakers as they sat on benches outside in the courtyard. The next day we had a chicken dinner to celebrate but, of course, no wine or cigars! The apostolic delegate from Rome also paid us a visit that summer. He gave the community a novena of nine extra recreation days during the centennial year, to be distributed at the discretion of the mother general. We clapped and clapped at such an innovative and very welcome gift!

I suppose someone who looked at this culture from the outside would think that it was very confining. Such requirements as needing permission to write a letter as well as to receive one unopened, make personal or even professional phone calls, receive guests in the parlour, acquire new articles of clothing and dispose of worn ones could all seem extremely oppressive. However, I do know that it was a very happy way of life and deeply joyful. Women formed profound relationships with each other and were able genuinely to recognize each other as sisters. Interestingly enough, although we all dressed the same and followed the same daily routine, the women in the congregation formed distinct personalities and would become formidable educators and individuals in their own right.

Some lines in Somerset Maugham's *The Painted Veil* express a little of what this apparent conformity really means. Recently, they came to mind again after I saw the film of the same name. The mother superior of a group of French nuns who staffed an orphanage in China, near Hong Kong, where a cholera plague was raging in the 1920s, responds to Kitty, the unfaithful wife of a husband who compels her to accompany him into a veritable hell, where she undergoes a conversion and is able to reassess her life.

> Remember that it is nothing to do your duty, that is demanded of you and is no more meritorious than to wash your hands when they are dirty; the only thing

> that counts is the love of duty; when love and duty are one, then grace is in you and you will enjoy a happiness which passes all understanding.[1]

Our lives in the IHM community were basically the same as those of women in all apostolic religious congregations approved by the Church. It is important to note that in the 1940s and '50s, women religious in apostolic congregations in the United States lived, for the most part, in unspoken and unreflected isolation from one another, as they had done for decades. They were intent on preserving and enhancing their own charisms and customs, even though they often had the same ministries of education, health care and social service as other congregations. No regional or national organizations existed to bring them together to discuss religious life, nor did they seem necessary. Professionally, through the National Catholic Education Association and the Catholic Health Association, for example, sisters met as educators or health-care professionals, but they did not meet as people who shared the same vocation.

Vocations had increased substantially in the wake of the Second World War, since there was an increasing demand for teachers in schools, nurses in hospitals, and social workers to care for the poor. Routinely, the young women were sent out to teach with the barest minimum of credentials, placed under the tutelage of seasoned sister supervisors for mentoring, and destined to complete their education through Saturday classes and many years of summer courses.

The primary mission of the IHM Sisters was education. Because of this mission, initial and continuing education was seen as a priority. Thus, each summer, the sisters returned "home" to the mother house or to our college in Detroit from their teaching missions. We were housed in the dormitories of the two large boarding schools on our property. Most summers, there would be as many as 900 of us. In addition to the joy of being with each other, and making the annual eight-day retreat, we took courses in theology from Jesuit and Dominican theologians (we had no IHM theologians at the time) and other subjects from IHM professors. A significant number of our sisters were sent away to other Catholic educational institutions to obtain master's and doctoral degrees very early in the history of the congregation.

A study of the educational history of religious congregations of women in the United States is replete with stories of how women religious who owned and staffed liberal arts colleges for women were sent to universities in the United States and Europe to obtain doctorates long before such ventures would have met with the approval of Church authorities.

I made first vows in 1948 and, together with all my classmates in the novitiate, went out on my first teaching mission. Most of us had taken fundamental teaching education classes and had done practice teaching in the parochial schools of Monroe under the guidance and direction of "master teachers." However, it would take these young fledgling teachers seventeen summers to obtain a college degree.

During the first months of my life as a young professed sister, my mother died. As she approached death, one of my brothers came to pick me up and drive me home to see her. It was April 10, 1948, almost three years since I had left home. As we pulled into the driveway, my father was waiting for me on the front steps. I remember looking at my mother through the half-open door of her bedroom. She was now very thin, but somehow very beautiful, younger even. There was a television set on the dresser; it was the first time I had seen one. A number of my sisters and brothers were there, and a nurse was in attendance. My family all went downstairs to give me time with my mother. I knelt next to her and held her hand. She was very happy to see me. At one point when she moaned ever so slightly, she looked at me with a faint smile and said, "I suppose that when the sisters are sick they don't utter a peep!" Despite her light remark, I knew she was close to death. Before long, a change came over her and the nurse told me to get the other members of the family. All of us gathered around her bed to pray. We had prayed only one decade of the rosary when she gently passed away. My father took her in his arms, saying, "I loved her so."

Because my mother had an aversion to funeral parlours, my father had her embalmed and laid out at home. In those days, IHM sisters never went into private homes, except for rare occasions such as the death of a parent. And so, none of my IHM sisters could come to view my mother's body or offer sympathy to my family. My religious superior told me, however, that I could stay with my family during this time. I was to stay in the library at the back of the house, but could come out briefly when there was some person that my father wished me to see.

At the funeral, I was not allowed to sit with my family; instead, I sat across the aisle with a large group of IHM sisters who were present. I sat at the end of the pew and watched my family process up the aisle behind the coffin. On the way out, after the liturgy, my father came over to me and placed my mother's wedding ring in my hand. It was a very special and touching moment. I would receive this same gold ring on the day of my final profession a few years later.

I was not allowed to go to the cemetery where my mother would be buried. Instead, I went back to one of the local convents, and my father and sisters and brothers came over after the burial. The superior served us Vernor's ginger ale and Oreo cookies. As a rare exception, I was allowed to join them. I am certain that after they left me they went home and had the kind of Irish wake that I have since attended when other family members have died. Those were and are important times, when we gather to tell stories, to share in the hospitality and generosity of neighbours and friends and, for certain, to drink something stronger than ginger ale.

Today, of course, all that rigidity and separation is long gone. However, in the late 1940s, it was common custom and fitting behaviour of sisters who had "left the world."

3

Forming for the Future Without Knowing It

During my second-year novitiate, I was sent to teach fourth grade in one of the parochial schools in Monroe. I came to the ministry with a college degree and a teacher's certificate, and I had done practice teaching in one of the grade schools in Detroit under the tutelage of an expert teacher. However, I still had to learn the art of classroom order, such as directing the children in and out of the coat room, the lunch room, the lavatories and the parish church for Mass; how to keep desks in order; and a thousand other practicalities that make for good order and set the ambiance for learning. None of these important experiences was a part of practice teaching. Entering into the classroom of a skilled teacher for one or two hours and teaching a reading or math lesson was just one tiny aspect of being in charge of over 40 animated youngsters. Because of a variety of circumstances, when I arrived in that fourth-grade classroom, I was their third teacher of the school year, and it was only January. This situation was, I soon learned, a recipe for disaster.

That year I learned something about the meaning of reconciliation from an unexpected source. Bernard Rupp was a lively and precocious boy. I was unable to control or interest him for more than about ten minutes. In utter desperation, I took him out into the hall, looked down at him with the most severe countenance I could muster and demanded in a threatening voice, "Bernard, what are you going to do about your behaviour?" He hung his head, shifted from one foot to another and responded solemnly, "I'm just a bum, sister." After three such imperious demands on my part met with the same response, I said, "But what are you going to *do* about your 'bumdom'?" This time, wisely realizing that words were not going to remedy the situation, he looked up at me very solemnly and somewhat shyly with his wide brown eyes and said, "Well, [long pause] I could kiss you."

This response completely undid me. I realized that this was likely the way that he responded to reprimands from his parents. Out of the mouths of babes, I thought, remembering these words of Jesus: "unless you become as a little child ...." I hope that if by some chance Bernard Rupp reads these words, he will be happy to learn that as a fourth grader he taught me an invaluable lesson that I never forgot ... even if he has.

My superiors, realizing that I had no talent for coping with younger children, wisely assigned me to teaching high school. Tenth graders were a joy and a stimulating challenge. And best of all, the students and I got along well. However, my somewhat casual approach to classroom decorum was challenged one evening in November when I heard two very seasoned sisters talking in the kitchen. "Today, someone sighed out loud when I gave out an assignment," said Sister Ann Virginia to Sister Fidelis. I marvelled at such a statement, reflecting that it was unlikely that my classroom would ever be silent enough to even *hear* a sigh! "Sandra Timlin," Sister Ann Virginia had replied to the sighing student, "some day in the future, a sigh of disapproval to a request of your employer just might cost you your job!"

I decided then and there that a change had to happen in my classroom, even though it was already November. Norm Masters was a hulking sophomore on the school football team (he later played professional football with the Green Bay Packers in Wisconsin). He sat in the last row of desks with one long leg almost always in the aisle. "Foot in," I gestured. "Foot in." A moment later, the long leg appeared again. "Foot in," I repeated.

"What's the matter, Sister?" Norm asked with exasperation. "Yesterday, last week and last month it's okay but today it's 'Foot in. Foot in.'"

Seeking a word of wisdom, I consulted Sister Ann Virginia, who pointed out that any rules of decorum you did not set in September could not easily be imposed three months later. In how many other situations in life does this wise advice not apply?!

During my second year of teaching, I returned home to the mother house at Christmastime to make my final vows and receive the gold ring as a sign of that profession. Returning to school, my students noticed. One of the boys said it best: "Hey, Sister, in for life?"

By the late 1940s and early 1950s, a major educational shift in religious education was stirring on two fronts. Already a spiritual awakening was occurring, promoted by Dominican priests who re-edited the *Summa Theologica* into three volumes and made the teaching of St. Thomas Aquinas available to the laity. Even more powerfully, the liturgical movement, which had begun in Europe, was taking hold, first at St. John's Seminary in Collegeville, Minnesota, and then in one religious congregation after another. This shift was having powerful effects on our spirituality, which became more deeply rooted in the prayer of the Church. Closer to home, the movement to improve the education of women religious was gathering its own momentum.

The sister formation movement, with which I was to become intimately involved, was one of the first ways in which religious congregations of women in the United States began to work together. In general, as I mentioned earlier, congregations remained largely isolated from one another. We had become professionals and ran large institutions of the Church in efficient and effective ways. A good deal of this success had to do with the way we structured and lived our lives.

As IHM teachers in the immense parochial school system, we lived very simply in convents owned by the parishes and received very little recompense—a stipend more than a salary. We sent as much of our earnings as possible back "home" to the mother house. Through this common life and frugal use of monies, we and all sisters were able to maintain our mother houses, take care of the elderly and infirm, and provide for the years of formation that the young women entering our congregations required. During the Depression, parishes sometimes curtailed even these meagre salaries, since the parents of many students in the parochial schools could not afford to pay tuition. For these families, public schools were not an option. To protect the faith of Catholics in a country built on the foundation of separation of church and state, the U.S. bishops had convened plenary councils in Baltimore throughout the nineteenth century to deal with a number of pastoral challenges for the nation's Catholics, many of whom were immigrants. The bishops decided to establish parochial schools to preserve and teach the faith. Women religious became the workforce that enabled it to happen.

When I entered the IHM congregation in 1945, members received $45 per month for the academic year. As a young IHM, I heard older sisters recount that during the Depression it was the music teachers who were often the community breadwinners. Teaching and playing "Happy Farmer" over and over to young aspiring musicians after school and most of Saturday became an important source of income in the strained economy of the late 1920s and 1930s. Many of the sisters were accomplished musicians. They offered members of choral groups, marching bands, and talented individuals an outstanding musical education. These young people performed with beauty and precision.

As a young sister, I heard Sister Mary Patrick Riley, an IHM council member in charge of education, relate a conversation she had had with one of the diocese's school superintendents. He had come to the mother house to discuss the matter of holding back the young sisters from teaching so they could complete their education before entering the classroom, a decision he disapproved of. For him, the problem was having to pay salaries for lay teachers, who until then had been few and far between in the parochial school system, rather than speeding up the education of the sisters.

When Monsignor arrived at the mother house, he was shown to the "priest's parlour." Such reception and visiting rooms for the clergy were always furnished with good taste—often, I must add, with beautiful pieces that had come to the community from the homes of deceased parents of the sisters or other benefactors. Monsignor looked around appreciatively and noted, somewhat smugly, that it appeared to him that "the sisters had done very well for themselves." "And *by* ourselves," came the smiling but swift reply of Sister Mary Patrick.

Indeed, it could be said that in many ways, orders of religious women were the guardians of religious culture of the Catholic Church in America. Sisters were generally loved by the Catholic people and were held in great esteem and affection. For thousands of children, the sisters showed the loving face of God. However, for the most part, they were expected to implement what the bishops and priests decided. The archives of almost every congregation of women holds stories not only of painful struggles but also of perspicacious ways in which they went beyond the image of the "good sister."

Although the broad outlines (and sometimes the details) of their lives were decided by the clergy, the women religious found ways in which to exercise leadership that seem remarkable even today. For example, Elizabeth Lange, a French-speaking Creole woman from Haiti, and Katherine Drexel, a wealthy heiress from Pennsylvania, both founded religious congregations to educate African-Americans. They opened schools and colleges while confronting racism within the Catholic community. The Oblate Sisters of Providence, founded by Elizabeth Lange, were perceived as a scandal. A black woman in a religious habit was totally unacceptable in the nineteenth century and a shocking sight to the Catholics of Baltimore, many of whom were slave owners, including bishops and religious orders of both women and men.

In 1883, when a tornado ripped through Rochester, Minnesota, Mother Alfred Moes, a Franciscan sister whose difficulties with bishops were legion, lobbied the Mayo brothers, Charles and William, to staff a hospital if she would get it built. Although they were not interested at first, Mother prevailed. Today, the world-renowned Mayo clinic and St. Mary's Hospital in Rochester are a testimony to her indomitable spirit.

Another even more formidable reality in religious congregations prepared them to take up the challenge of the sister formation movement: the establishment of Catholic women's colleges and a dedication to the higher education of women. Even today, few people may realize the contribution to the public good of many women educated in nearly 200 such institutions across the country over the years. Many women who served and are serving in Congress, who have become high court judges, ambassadors, physicians, classical musicians, medical researchers, and even a U.S. brigadier-general and a Navy rear admiral are graduates of Catholic women's colleges. Today, for a variety of reasons, their number is fewer. Nevertheless, some distinguished Catholic women's colleges continue to impart Christian values and foster strong relationships among women. These colleges include Saint Mary's College in Notre Dame, Indiana; Trinity College in Washington, DC (now Trinity Washington University); College of Saint Elizabeth in New Jersey; Saint Mary-of-the-Woods College in Indiana; College of Saint Benedict in St. Joseph, Minnesota; the College of St. Catherine in St. Paul, Minnesota; and Marygrove College in Detroit.

Formidable women were behind the initiatives that brought these institutions into being. For example, through the extraordinarily far-sighted vision of Sister Antonio McHugh, CSJ, president of the College of St. Catherine, sisters were sent to all the best universities of Europe to study and obtain degrees. The college later produced Rhodes and Fulbright scholars and in 1937 qualified for a chapter of the Phi Beta Kappa honour society. It was the first Catholic college in the nation to achieve this recognition. Today, I am happy and proud to say that an IHM sister, Andrea J. Lee, is the president of the College of St. Catherine's and carries forward its remarkable heritage of excellence.

The women who took up the challenge of sister formation were themselves the products of such foresight in their own religious congregations.

In the IHM congregation, two general superiors, Mother Mechtildis McGrath and Mother Domitilla Donahue, got around the prohibition on women religious attending secular universities. With the characteristic shrewdness of the serpent and simplicity of the dove, these two superiors sent postulants to the University of Michigan to obtain college degrees that, as professed religious, they would not be allowed to receive. Others went to the University of Notre Dame, Fordham and Catholic University.

Commitment to higher education had long been a priority for the IHM congregation. Very early in its history, IHM sisters taught college courses at St. Mary's Academy in Monroe, and in 1907 a full four-year program leading to a bachelor of arts degree was established. In 1927, the Monroe college was moved to Detroit and named Marygrove.

The Sister Formation Movement

In the 1940s, innovative women religious were beginning to question the long years it took to obtain the degrees they needed to carry on their work. Sister Madeleva Wolff CSC, President of Saint Mary's College in South Bend, Indiana, and a powerful influence in the National Catholic Education Association (NCEA), to which the many teaching congregations of

Sisters in the United States belonged, was instrumental in the creation of a Teacher-Education section within the College and University Department of the NCEA. It was this initiative that first drew together leaders from religious congregations as well as superintendents of the parochial school system to discuss the problems and promise of education in the vast network of elementary and secondary high schools stretching across the country. Sister Madeleva's prophetic insights had already been at work in creating the first graduate school of theology for women in the United States in 1944. To get around the Church's prohibition of women pursuing degrees in theology, she found clerical allies who shared her vision and, with them, found ways to circumvent the obstacles that existed.

In the IHM congregation, attempts were being made to ensure that each young sister was fully prepared with a college degree before going out to teach. Sister Mary Patrick Riley, herself a consummate educator, was creative, tireless and sometimes outrageously innovative in her promotion and advocacy of this great dream. All of us in the IHM community recognized that, in many ways, she was larger than life and that she hoped that everyone else was as well.

When the NCEA met in Kansas City in 1952, she was to be on a panel in the Teacher-Education section to discuss Pius XII's *Counsel to Teaching Sisters*. Unable to attend due to a death in her family, she sent in her place Sister Mary Emil Penet, IHM, a teacher of philosophy in our nascent formation college at the mother house. And, as the saying goes, "The rest is history."

Sister Mary Emil's presentation and challenge to the sisters was twofold. First, she advocated replacing young sisters with lay teachers as the sisters pursued their degrees. Second, because no religious congregation could bring about this change on its own, she proposed that there be some kind of organizational unity among religious congregations engaged in education to confront the challenges that lay ahead. The sister formation movement, which would eventually have a crucial impact on religious life in the United States, was born.

The outcome of Sister Mary Emil's challenge was electric. It engendered an immediate response and spirited discussion. Women from a variety of congregations shared their experiences, transcended their congregational differences, found a common voice and initiated a movement that, for a decade, would unleash the creative energies of hundreds of women religious in unprecedented and unimagined ways.

The sisters who were to become the leaders and founders of this movement—Sister Mary Emil, along with Sister Annette Walters, CSJ, Sister Emmanuel Collins, OSF, and Rita Mary Bradley, CHM—were themselves outstanding women and educators. Through their efforts, major superiors of various orders were drawn together into a common enterprise that initially raised the ire of many pastors and bishops who saw no reason for such a program and did not want to spend the money to hire lay teachers. In their eyes, getting degrees over the course of many years had not hindered the growth and effective influence of the parochial school system in the past, and they saw no reason why the system should change for the future.

However, in a short time, the movement took hold, and sister education became an established fact. Besides creating juniorates during which young sisters would be educated, the movement published the *Sister Formation Bulletin*, a quarterly newsletter that became a major catalyst of theological reflection and conversation. Articles written by such rising European scholars as Yves Congar, Henri de Lubac, Bernard Haring and Karl Rahner made their way into the convents of women religious a decade before the Second Vatican Council began. In this way, not only the young sisters but also the active sisters in schools and hospitals were being formed and challenged by the theology that would become one of the bases of the Council documents.

For the next decade, this grassroots movement drew together women from dozens of congregations in a common cause and commitment. History may look upon this movement as only a brief moment of ten years—a mere "blip on the screen," but the movement was and is one of those shining lights that streaks across the sky, lighting up the dark and, in its passage, giving us a glimmer of what lies behind, beneath and before the surrounding darkness. The sister formation movement would eventually have tremendous implications. Religious women, more than any other group in the Church, would be prepared to receive the teaching of Vatican II.

Formation Mistress

In the late 1940s, as a recipient of the early thinking around sister education and because of the far-reaching vision of Sister Mary Patrick, I was sent to begin graduate studies at the doctoral level at Saint Mary's College, the only place in the United States, as I noted earlier, where women could earn such a degree in theology. (Like most IHM sisters at that time, I earned my master's degree over the course of many summers.)

A master's program was also available over a five-year summer school program. The campus was filled with women from a variety of congregations taking advantage of this innovative endeavour. I marvelled at the variety of religious customs and costumes that unfolded before my eyes during the liturgy each morning. Some sisters put on extra sleeves, others pulled them down over their hands, while the Mercy Sisters wore an added train that flowed behind them. However, it was the School Sisters of Notre Dame who most intrigued me. With a very deft gesture, they would cause their large extra veil to fall gracefully and cover their entire face after they received communion, while their long sleeves would extend like a muff and completely cover their hands. As IHMs we had only the practice of wearing a long black cloak to cover our royal blue habit when we left the convent for any outside business.

The doctoral program at St. Mary's had only a few participants and required a long residency over a number of years.

The major text of study for doctoral students, reflecting the re-emergence of Dominican influence, was the *Summa Theologica* of St. Thomas Aquinas. I loved the architectural structure of the *Summa* as well as grappling with the metaphysical philosophy that gave reason to the faith. I also took courses in moral theology, scripture, patristics, hagiography and canon law. I was introduced as well to ascetical and mystical theology and, on my own, began to read the Rhineland and Carmelite mystics. Books of this nature were, for the most part, in the locked section of IHM convent libraries, because, as we were told, ascetical theology (the way of the virtues) rather than mystical theology (the way of contemplation) was the kind of spirituality to which we were called as active religious.

My scriptural studies at St. Mary's were influenced by form and redaction criticism, the process of making judgments about the historical background, literary form and authorship of biblical texts. Pius XII's encyclical *Divino Afflante Spiritu* reopened forms of interpretation that had been closed to biblical scholars for many years. The encyclicals *Mystici Corporis* and *Mediator Dei* made deep and profound impressions on me, and I grew into a great love of the Church as the Mystical Body of Christ and of the liturgy, through which the life of the Church is most deeply expressed. This love, which in time would be so marked by both light and deep shadow, became and remains the foundation of my spiritual life.

During the summer, I also took advantage of the courses offered as part of the liturgical theology program at the University of Notre Dame. Here, I experienced the dynamism of Benedictine monks and teachers such as Godfrey Diekmann, Dom Vitry, and a host of others. It challenges the imagination today to picture a liturgical picnic, with female and male student religious in the various cuts and colours of habits that identified the many religious congregations. We would crowd onto a school bus, each with our lunch and our *Liber Usualis*, the four-inch book of Gregorian chants for the various liturgical seasons, feast days and Sundays edited by the Benedictine monks of Solesmes. Instead of the "Old McDonald had a farm ..." variety of songs that normally accompanied such outings in the secular world, try to imagine us calling out for the *Introit* from the Christmas Mass at dawn, the *communio* for All Saints' Day, the *Sequence for Pentecost* or even the *Dies Irae* from the Mass of the Dead!

In my years of study at St. Mary's, there were no formal courses in ecclesiology (the theology of the Church). I suspect this was the case because there was no tract on the Church in the *Summa*. However, in the summer after I finished my studies at St. Mary's, again with the nudging of Sister Mary Patrick, I went "across the road" to the University of Notre Dame, where I took several courses and began to read and study the seminal works of Yves Congar, Henri de Lubac, Karl Rahner and other representatives of the so-called *Nouvelle Théologie*, whose works had been translated into English. Thus, my ecclesiological education began in depth. Even though these writers were, for a time, held in great suspicion and in some instances deprived of their teaching privileges, they all became important *periti* or experts of the Second Vatican Council that was to be convened in 1962, which was just a few short years in the future.

Being away from the IHM community all those years was in many ways like an extended retreat. Nonetheless, I was expected to live my religious life just as strictly as though I were living in an IHM convent. When I finished my studies, I returned "home" to join the staff of the sister formation teaching faculty on the Monroe campus of our congregational college. At the same time, I was working with the novice mistress. Having experience in both the novitiate and the college brought me close to the inevitable tensions that arose between spiritual and intellectual formation in those early years. I found myself at the heart of a very real conflict that continues to exist in some ways even now. Fledgling college programs for religious initially could not afford to last four years, since sisters were needed in the ever-expanding schools of the 1950s. Consequently, second-year novices were given a full load of study that left not enough time for deeper spiritual formation. On the other hand, first-year canonical novices, who were not allowed to study but had to concentrate on spiritual formation, were called upon to do all the manual work of the mother house "charges" or chores, which had previously been shared with the second-year novices. In many ways, a "lose-lose" situation developed, until the built-in tensions were resolved by giving more time for the young sisters to stay at the mother house so the novitiate could be what it truly was meant to be, as well as to design a juniorate in which these same young women could give themselves to study in an atmosphere conducive to its meaning and its own spirituality.

Another tension that arose was the content of the intellectual formation the young sisters were receiving. Teaching young religious to become critical thinkers at a time when spiritual formation did not tend in this direction was bound to provoke some tensions. Nonetheless, the young women formed in those years (the 1950s) learned to be critical thinkers in the best sense. They, along with other young religious across the country who were shaped by the sister formation movement, were more than adequately prepared to respond to the challenges of Vatican II. (It must be said, though, that in the 1940s and early 1950s very few of us saw any need for the Church or religious life to radically change. We were successful. Our work was bearing fruit. Novitiates were full and the wider American culture increasingly respected Catholic institutions.)

I became novice directress in 1962. This was for me an incredible privilege and task.

In the IHM congregation, the novice directress (originally called the novice mistress) was called "the second foundress of the community." She was to instill into young candidates the spirit as well as the letter of the congregation, and was the person solely charged with this awesome task.

As I worked with the novices, their insistent and insightful questions pushed little wedges of truth into my mind that I could not ignore. Nor could looking over my glasses and wagging my finger, admonishing the person in question, "Little sister, you came to *join* a community, not to *found* one," assuage the growing awareness that a new reality was breaking in on us, insistently and irrevocably. The novices were not just going to hear and accept an uncritical reading and study of the rule and follow it, especially if it did not make sense to them. I would often say to the general superior that it would take a whole instruction period to tell the novices what the rule did *not* mean. For example, article two of our constitutions stated that "the spirit of the congregation consists in self-abnegation and renouncement of self-will." My attempts to rephrase these concepts in positive terms were laborious. At the end of one of these attempts, one of the novices would inevitably ask, "Why doesn't it just say that, then?" Moreover, in speaking of the role of the novice directress, the rule was every bit as stark: "The novice [directress] will have failed in her duty if she does not make certain that the novices die to their own will and opinion."

As I look back over my own IHM life, the fourteen years that I spent in formation ministry were truly the most blessed and rewarding in many ways. I learned more from these generous young women than I was able to convey to them through my instruction.

II

The Bright Colours of Vatican II

1

Renewing the Vision

The events of the Second Vatican Council would irrevocably alter the landscape of life in the Catholic Church. In an especially dramatic way, this would be true of religious life in general and of religious life in the United States in particular.

The impetus for the Council did not originate in the United States. It grew from the experience of the churches of Europe as they were tested in the crucible of war and disaster. It was in Europe that the seeds of Vatican II were planted through a renewal of biblical studies, a fresh view of Thomistic theology, and the liturgical movement. These new insights would find fertile ground in the United States.

In the early 1950s, Pius XII urged women religious, including teachers and health-care professionals, to update their lives in the light of the changing culture. In response to his summons, women religious in the United States began to hold conferences to discuss how they could be a greater force and influence in society. Leaders such as Cardinal Suenens of Belgium provided an urgent voice as well. Later, he was to be a champion of Church renewal at key junctures of the Council. His urgent request, which he wrote to women religious in *The Nun in the World* (1962), had a major influence on the renewal. In the foreword, which sums up the content of the book, Cardinal Suenens wrote,

> We hope to examine the place and the mission of the nuns in the Church in terms of the world as it is today. This study is of interest to the whole Church for the nun is called to play a leading role .... We shall at the same time bring to light the chief problems that concern the whole field of pastoral work.

Suenens's successor, Godfried Danneels, described him as "an excellent weather forecaster who knew from which direction the wind was blowing in the Church, and an experienced strategist who realized that he could not change the wind's destiny but could set the sails to suit it."

After Vatican II, in spite of the initial reluctance of American religious congregations to follow the suggestions of Pius XII, women religious again took up the challenge, this time with greater enthusiasm. In doing so, we reflected the American tendency to embrace new experiences, to explore new frontiers. Like others in our culture, we were confident that we could be part of something new and better. In addition, because the call to renewal had come from the Church, the Pope and the bishops, we religious (obedient as always) took it very seriously and, I believe, were more affected by it than any other group in the Church was. At the same time, we had to deal with the legacy of congregations of women acting independently of one another well into the 1950s to preserve what they guarded as "their own spirit."

While I was entirely happy in the traditional model of religious life as it had been lived for hundreds of years, I was open to the coming changes. The rumours of a new way of looking at the Church, the world and religious life began to flow out of historic meetings in Rome in the 1960s and make inroads into our lives. We read and internalized the Vatican documents written by the "new" theologians.

To use the framework of Bernard Lonergan, I would say that for me the change from the traditional model of religious life to the Vatican II model was a process of conversion. It involved a real change in world view, in horizon. It was a conversion that took place in different ways and on many levels.

Of course, a kind of conversion was going on in the rest of the world as well. The culture of what we had called "modern times" began to collapse. The Church, which had strongly resisted the culture of modernity for centuries, was beginning to question itself from within. It was facing a change of ideologies within itself and in the world. The Church had to face the emergence of the behavioural sciences, as well as the increasing interdependence of the world.

When Pope John XXIII called the Second Vatican Council, he said that it came as a "sudden inspiration" while he was preparing a talk during the Church Unity Octave. "What could I do for unity?" he wondered. Moreover, he was a pastoral man, more concerned with experience than expertise. The wind that blew through the windows of the Vatican proved to be more than a gentle breeze.

The documents of Vatican II changed our thinking on a range of important topics: revelation and tradition; the nature of ministry and of the Church; the meaning of human freedom, God's will and vocation; individual and social conscience; personal responsibility; and the Church's relationship to the world. All of these topics raised "a million questions" at once.

Perfectae Caritatis (*Decree on the Adaptation and Renewal of Religious Life*) called us to renew our charism—that is, the original inspiration or gift given to the founders of our religious order. The basic inspiration for many congregations, often quite prophetic, had become submerged and lost under prescriptions that hindered rather than enhanced the purposes for which they were founded, though we did not recognize it then. In the light of Vatican II, our sense of how the Holy Spirit moved in our communities was reversed. The charism of a religious congregation was given to the founder *for* the Church, not *from* the Church to the founder. This insight reversed the order of things that had made it possible for the clergy to preach about our congregation on its centennial celebration while the sisters sat outside. We began to see ourselves *as* ourselves—women in the Church empowered by our own Spirit-given charisms and called by God to minister with our brother priests as collaborators in the great work of evangelization.

Our central conviction about living in obedience to God's will was also challenged. Prior to the Council, as I mentioned earlier, our notion of God's will was a static one. God had a plan: a blueprint for the Church and for the lives of each one of us. Our task was to discover that will, which we believed to be outside of us. After Vatican II, a new concept of God's will began to emerge, due in great part to renewed New Testament ecclesiology. The Spirit had been given to the whole Church; all persons were responsible for its mission. The role of leadership and authority became one of listening: leaders were to interpret the movements of God's will within the Church, to focus, and to discern those movements in order to take the Church forward and to promote the reign of God, which was one of justice and peace. Obedience now demanded personal responsibility and the formation of conscience that befits a mature Christian.

For us, it meant paying attention to our own experience and believing it—owning it. We were called to be more present to the world, to be summoned to wider ministries, especially to the poor and oppressed. This approach answered the challenge of *Gaudium et Spes*, "that the joys, sorrows, hopes and fears of the whole human family were also the joys, sorrows, hopes and fears of the Church." We wanted to respond to the more particular call of Pope Paul VI to women religious—"How will you answer the cry of the poor?"—as well as to his insistence that we give up some traditional works in order to answer this call. Our response to these challenges brought us into immediate conflict with Church leaders.

These new intellectual insights touched our relationship with God to the core. It asked a death of us—a *kenosis*. It led us into a cloud of unknowing, and at the same time caused us to intensify and purify our relationship to God.

However, this was only the beginning. More seriously, we had to ask, "How do we *live* in the foci of these new insights?" We had begun the process of repainting our image of religious life.

For me, the experience of working on our first revised constitutions in light of the Council, whose documents were already accessible to us even though the Council was still in session, gave me a sense of the depth of the process of conversion we would be called to. Our general chapter of 1960 had called for a rule revision committee. Of the hundreds of hours spent on the initial revision of our constitutions, one meeting in particular remains etched in my mind. Reflecting on the experience of the Council fathers as they sought to understand the nature of the Church and its role in the modern world, we were struck over and over by the pastoral tone of the documents, the rich biblical foundation, the lack of "anathemas" that had marked so much previous legislation. As a result, the committee came to the sobering conclusion that the structure and articulation of our lives as religious, spelled out in the constitutions that had formed and guided IHM sisters for generations, could not be "patched up," changed here and there. We had to acknowledge that the constitutions no longer adequately expressed who we were and who we were called to be in a Church that no longer separated itself from the world. We had to come to terms with a Church that acknowledged the universal call to holiness and recognized the vocation of all the baptized in the furthering of its mission. As a result, the committee set out to prepare new constitutions. It would end up taking over 20 years. After several drafts that reflected consultations with the whole congregation over a number of years, a new and rich text, rooted in scripture, the Council documents and our own tradition, was given final approval by Rome on November 10, 1989.

2

General Superior

Our congregation prepared for the 1966 general chapter just as the Council ended. (General chapters normally met every six years to deliberate on the life and mission of the congregation, as well as to elect the women who would serve as leaders for the next six years.) The winds of change were already blowing about and in our work of revising the constitutions.

The professed members of the congregation voted for the members of the chapter from across the community. This group of 46 women would elect the general superior and her council, as well as deliberate on all the proposals for change that had been sent to the chapter by the members at large. The election was carried out in great solemnity by secret ballot and in the presence of the bishop. Away from the larger community, the delegates gathered in a small chapel in our academy attached to the mother house. I was an elected member of that gathering.

On the morning of June 18, 1966, I left the novitiate in a state of mind not unlike the one I was in when I left home for the convent 21 years earlier—lacking a strong sense of what lay ahead. I had not seriously imagined that I might never return to the novitiate, which had been my home for fourteen years, but at the same time, I must say that some rumours about election had filtered into my secluded and sequestered life with the novices. I discovered later, as I began to attend meetings with general superiors across the country, that I had already known and worked with many of them in the sister formation movement in the pre-Council years. It occurred to me that the sisters who had had first-hand experience of change through their involvement in the sister formation movement would be logical choices for congregational leaders.

At the solemn gathering of delegates that June morning, in the presence of Joseph Breitenback, the presiding bishop, I was elected general superior of the Monroe IHM congregation. As I heard my name called, a wave of light-headedness swept over me. After what seemed to me to be a long and deafening silence, I felt a poke in the back.

"Go up there," someone said.

"Up where?" I wondered.

The bishop looked in my direction, and somehow I managed to reach the sanctuary, where he asked me whether I accepted the election. I must have said yes, though I hardly remember. The pen he gave me to sign the official election document shook so violently in my hand that I could not write.

"My hand won't work," I whispered.

"Just make a mark," he answered with a smile. I have always wanted to look back at that document and see how "Sister M. Benedicta" looks—close to unreadable, I suspect.

According to the IHM constitutions at that time, after the election of the general superior, all the delegates were to come up one by one, then kneel and kiss her hand as a mark of their respect and obedience. I knew instantly and instinctively that this was not what I needed from these women who had entrusted me with leadership. And so I made my first change as general superior and asked them to give me what I most longed for and needed—the kiss of peace. I cherish the memory of Mother Teresa McGivney, a beloved former general superior, whispering in my ear, "I am glad that I did not waste my vote." Her words remained with me and gave me courage in the years to follow.

Following the vote for the general superior, four other women were elected as councillors and a sixth as treasurer. The six of us did not know each other well, and we had not spoken to each other about the possibility of being elected. Indeed, such conversations were forbidden under the rubric of "politicking." While I suppose, inevitably, there were some such conversations, in fact we were exhorted to leave choices of leadership to the Holy Spirit and to pray for enlightenment.

As the day of election came to a close, the belongings of those of us called to congregational leadership had already been moved to the second floor C corridor of the mother house, where the councillors and general superior traditionally had their cells, as our rooms were called. Late in the evening, Sister Marmion (Jane Johnson), who had been elected treasurer, approached me in the corridor outside of our rooms. Where could she find a pair of shoelaces? Knowing that I had been living in the mother house, she presumed I would know the answer to such a simple request. However, I was as ignorant as she was. After all, I had been living in the novitiate, two whole corridors and a wing away. Nevertheless, wanting to be helpful, I suggested that Sister Alexaida, whom I knew to be in charge of the common press (actually a cupboard) where such items as shoelaces, toothbrushes and soap could be procured, would very likely be found down by the sewing rooms (another corridor and a wing away) after Mass and breakfast the next morning. With a look of utter incredulity mixed with incomprehension, Sister Marmion shook her head ever so slightly and said, "This place is barbaric!" As the next few years would prove, it did not take long for Sister Marmion, among other, weightier tasks, to go about the work of humanizing the mother house. Small community rooms, kitchenettes and laundry facilities began to appear on each long stretch of corridor. And—marvel of marvels—not one but *two* ice-cold water fountains appeared in the main corridor of the mother house.

Today, as I look back more than 40 years later, I continue to be amazed that the women with whom I ministered in leadership during that decade not only formed a creative and dedicated team but also laboured together to bring to reality the most sweeping changes that our congregation had ever encountered. Over the years we were in office, we came to know each other in and through our common commitment and mandate we had to implement the chapter proceedings. We were able, through some daunting times and events, to forge deep friendships that have lasted to this very day. Today, electing practical strangers to work together would strike many as truly unenlightened and perhaps even dangerous. However, this practice reflected a different time and a different religious culture that in some ways has, unfortunately, forever disappeared. I say "unfortunately" only because, in retrospect, the election process during the course of our history seemed to reflect the congregation's more deliberate seeking out of the guidance of the Holy Spirit in prayer than do today's somewhat secular procedures. On the other hand, the more open conversations we have now to solicit and learn about persons willing to take on positions of leadership surely speak well of our sense of responsibility across the congregation.

The election of community leaders had been preceded by a silent and solemn retreat for the delegates. Providentially, and perhaps even prophetically, we were especially fortunate to have Father Bernard Haring as the retreat director. He had been a valued consultant to us during the years that we revised our rule. As a member of that committee, I had been sent to consult with him at Loyola College in Chicago. I was in full habit. I met Father Haring in the afternoon. We went for a walk on the campus, and ended up sitting on a bench where he opened with a question. "When," he said, referring to my IHM headpiece and the large flexiline collar, "are you going to get rid of that helmet and shield?" It was a startling beginning to our first conversation.

As a Redemptorist, Father Haring was well aware of our spirit and of the Second Vatican Council's insistence that religious women and men return to the spirit of their founders and interpret their charism in the light of the times. Moreover, as a *periti* to the Council, he was deeply committed to its teaching, upon which he had had a profound influence. A special concern of Father Haring's was the renewal of religious life. For him, this meant in particular the life of prayer, which would give religious not only grounding to implement the challenges of the Council, but also the courage to move in unknown and uncharted directions. For this reason, as well as due to our own reading of the Council documents, delegates were committed to the spiritual renewal of the congregation as our first priority. Indeed, the preamble to the chapter enactments of 1966 clearly states that intention:

> We, the members of the 1966 General Chapter of the Sisters, Servants of the Immaculate Heart of Mary, recognizing that our principal responsibility is the spiritual renewal of the congregation according to the guidelines given by Vatican II, do hereby resolve to consider all proposals submitted to the Chapter in the light of Conciliar principles ....

The preamble in its entirety sounded all the notes that would echo throughout the years to come: a sense of courage and a desire to remain united, yet at the same time hold respect for individual freedom and responsibility. We clearly saw ourselves as implementing something that the Church had asked of us.

The chapter of 1966 lasted from June 20 to the end of July. We discussed and debated 172 proposals. Of these, 109 were passed as enactments, the majority of which were to be implemented by the general government—in reality, the general superior and her council. Though the congregation as a whole had taken giant steps in the previous decade towards more frank and open conversation about its life and mission, the chapter itself carried out its business according to parliamentary procedure using Robert's Rules of Order. As the canonically elected general superior, I presided. What happened the very first morning as we began the deliberations must surely have given delegates cause for wonder at their choice of a leader. As the merits of a particular proposal were being discussed. I was dutifully trying to call on each person whose hand was raised. I was a bit startled and uncomprehending when Sister Mary Emil, with her deep and solemn voice, called the question. (In Robert's Rules of Order, to call the question means to cease the discussion and take a vote.)

"Have you a question, sister?" I asked.

The next day, a parliamentarian was appointed. Fortunately for my successors, the days of Robert's Rules of Order have long since given way to more collaborative and reflective ways of deliberating.

3

Detroit on the Move

We were fortunate to begin the process of renewal in an archdiocese with a remarkable leader, John Cardinal Dearden. He had come from Pittsburgh with a reputation for being a strict enforcer of the law, and was sometimes referred to as "Iron John." However, at the Vatican Council, Cardinal Dearden was a member of the commission that drafted *Lumen Gentium* (*Dogmatic Constitution on the Church*). As a result, he underwent a profound shift of consciousness and returned to Detroit deeply converted not only to *Lumen Gentium*'s conciliar theology but also to its implementation. To assist him in this momentous task, he appointed several auxiliary bishops, including Thomas Gumbleton, Kenneth Untener and Joseph Imesch, all of whom would continue to exemplify and implement the Council in remarkable and creative ways, though not without struggle, opposition and misinterpretation. Cardinal Dearden was also immensely influential and respected beyond the Archdiocese of Detroit: in 1966 he was elected the first president of the National Conference of Catholic Bishops (now the United States Conference of Catholic Bishops).

Among the pastoral writings of Bishop Ken Untener is an essay in *The Practical Prophet* entitled "Cardinal Dearden: A Gentleman of the Church."

> The gift of Cardinal Dearden was that when he realized that a thing was true, though clear out of his ken, he was able to take it in. He saw clearly what he saw but knew there was more to be seen. He was open to questions not of his own making. He was humble enough to wonder sometimes if he was right. He was secure enough to go with insight that sometimes made him wonder."[2]

From the outset we experienced the Cardinal's trust in us. As a newly elected general superior and council, we went to see him to ask for his blessing on our term of office. He talked about the importance of the Vatican Council and of the challenges that faced us in our implementation of its call. At the end of the visit, he said that he fully trusted us in the mandate we had received from the community and had only one request of us in our work of renewal.

What could that request be? I wondered.

"Do not ask me any questions," he said.

We interpreted his comment to mean that he had confidence in us both to understand and to carry out the directives of the Council. His words gave us a great feeling of courage and freedom. We felt we were being trusted and treated with respect. His support gave us the confidence to go ahead and do among ourselves what he was hoping to do in the whole diocese, of which, he told us, we were a most important and influential part.

Archbishop Dearden was made a cardinal in 1969. One of his first actions was to form a pastoral council in the archdiocese to implement Vatican II in many areas of the life of the Church. He was fully committed to the challenge of Vatican II, and was convinced that all the members of the Church were called not only to scrutinize the "signs of the times," but also to signal that all initiatives were to be deferred to the clergy, as they had been in the past. It was a challenging and innovative exercise of collegiality, which I believe he saw as both a hope and possibility for the Catholic Church across the country. The pastoral council was completely inclusive and composed predominantly of lay persons, though there were religious and priests as well. It was a wonderfully fruitful and creative time in the archdiocese. As a member of the pastoral council, I had my first experience of ministering outside the framework of religious life.

The decade of the 1960s in the United States, as we already knew, demanded courage in the midst of momentous social change. John F. Kennedy, the first Catholic president, had been elected in 1960 and assassinated in 1963. The civil rights movement galvanized the moral conscience of many in the country, and our sisters became involved on a number of levels. At least two of them had taken part in the historic march in Selma in 1965 in support of the civil rights movement. Before the end of the decade, we would witness the assassinations of Martin Luther King and Senator Robert Kennedy, as well as the murders of several black children and civil rights workers, both black and white, in the south.

Closer to home, racial uprisings in 1967 plunged the city of Detroit into an experience that has forever marked it. Many sisters ministered in schools and lived in convents situated at the heart of the uprising. They did not flee but remained committed to their neighbourhoods and to the people to whom they ministered. Our consciousness was heightened regarding the challenge and the blight of racism in a dramatic way.

My father still lived in the big house on the west side of Detroit where we had all grown up. His unmarried sister, Julia (Aunt Lu), lived with him.

The violence and destruction of uprising erupted in that former white middle-class neighbourhood, and my father was in the thick of it. My brothers and sisters tried to no avail to convince him and Aunt Lu to come to one of their homes. "These are my neighbours," my father would say. "They cannot flee, and neither will I."

One morning when I called the house and asked about him, Aunt Lu (they were both in their 80s) responded that he was outside.

"Doing what?" I asked.

"Talking to those soldiers in the tanks," she replied.

The federal troops had moved in!

I often visited my father, who was quite frail by this time, his memory somewhat impaired, although still very alert. His neighbours looked after him very gently. Insisting that he wanted to go to the golf club for "nine holes," he would sometimes start out down the street. When his neighbours would spot him, one or another would take him for a short car ride to distract him and then return him home, the golf club forgotten. Once a week, my sisters and brothers, with their husbands and wives, would gather together at the house for dinner. Monsignor Markey (Uncle Harold) often joined them.

One day when I visited, I brought some chicken and biscuits. I tried to entice my father to eat, but he resisted. Holding out the biscuits, I said, "Dad, *I* made the biscuits." His face lit up. He sat forward on the big chair, put up both hands and said with great pride, mixed with some incredulity, "You've been made a bishop?!" I did not disabuse him of this startling news. It did get him to eat, after all!

A particularly painful experience for us as a congregation was the withdrawal of IHM sisters from the teaching staff of St. Raymond's school in the Archdiocese of Detroit in September 1971. The sisters' attempts to include social issues in the religion program, especially the eradication of racial attitudes, caused grave concerns within the parish council as well as among many parents. People were concerned about the prospect of black children enrolling in the school, and feared that black families moving into the area might cause property values to fall. A number of painful meetings and encounters revealed an impasse from which further progress was impossible at that time. It seemed to the sisters that to be true to what they had committed themselves to do, they would regretfully have to leave the school. The incident resulted in a good deal of publicity, both in the local newspapers and on television. It was a painful experience on every level that illustrated how fraught with difficulty would be any attempts to integrate neighbourhoods and schools.

As the 1960s drew to a close, many of our sisters, influenced by the peace movement, joined in the protests against the war in Vietnam. But, most seriously, we were challenged in the fall of 1970 by the passage of what was called Proposal C. The Michigan legislature passed a bill that resulted in the withholding of significant tax dollars from Catholic education. Without this funding, over 40 schools in the Archdiocese were closed. The Cardinal pleaded with us not to leave the diocese, in spite of the fact that many sisters were left without ministries as a result of the closures. At the same time, bishops from other parts of the country were inviting us to come their way. "Remember me when you come into your kingdom" were the playful but pleading words of one bishop who wrote from a poor diocese in the southwest. At the same time, Cardinal Dearden began to establish new forms of religious education unconnected to the parochial schools. Within our own congregation, Sister Johnice, IHM, and Sister Elizabeth, IHM, two very talented sisters, established the Pius XII Institute. Through it, they initiated a whole new and inventive course of study for preparing religious educators, both lay and religious.

The combination of the pastoral council and the passage of Proposal C led many sisters to leave our traditional ministries in parochial schools and work directly with the poor in the inner cities, with Aboriginal people on reservations, as well as in Latin America and Africa. Sisters prepared through the Pius XII Institute, obtaining master's degrees in scripture and theology from other educational facilities. They were joined by countless lay women leaders, who eventually replaced the sisters as directors of religious education and pastoral associates in parishes. Other sisters were led into ministries among the elderly, prisoners, migrants, the black community and Aboriginal people. We began to see that the number of ways to fulfill our educational mission had increased widely; this mission was, in fact, inseparable from the call of the Council to work for justice. Spacious convents had been relinquished as schools closed and were turned into parish offices. The sisters lived among the people in neighbourhood homes. Religious habits gave way to secular dress, while the creation of new forms of prayer and community life that energized the faith sharing and life of religious replaced monastic practices and structured prayer. Heightened social consciousness motivated many to challenge unjust political and economic structures at home and abroad.

The calls to justice were clear and numerous. The ambience in the archdiocese and the spirit engendered by our 1966 chapter and our new constitutions gave us a mandate to respond to these calls and to embrace the joys and sufferings of the world around us. We, along with many other women religious, took part in questioning our government and its policies, especially after the Watergate scandals were revealed in 1972 and President Nixon resigned.

4

A Time of Light and a Time of Darkness

Before the start of the 1966 chapter, we sensed that the post–Vatican II context of religious life would bring about radical shifts in both ministries and lifestyle. We had come to a new understanding of ourselves as women religious in what we knew was a swiftly changing culture. Paragraph two of *Perfectae Caritatis* became a guiding principle and lodestone for the changes we would make as well as the new directions we would take:

> Since the religious life is intended above all else to lead those who embrace it to an imitation of Christ and union with God through the profession of the evangelical counsels, the fact must be honestly faced that even the most desirable changes made on behalf of contemporary needs will fail of their purpose unless a renewal of spirit gives life to them.

It was for this reason that we committed ourselves most especially to the spiritual renewal of the congregation. Three areas in particular became foundational in this regard: the development of a house of prayer; the influence of the Ignatian retrieval of directed retreats; and the training and formation of sisters in spiritual direction and theological education, which would ground us as women in the Church in a postmodern world. We also hoped that spiritual renewal would be the foundation for other practical changes in our lives and ministries.

House of Prayer

The establishment of a house of prayer, one of the first enactments of the chapter, was of profound interest to me. When I first returned from my doctoral studies and my long immersion in theology and prayer in the contemplative ambience of Saint Mary's College, I thought (probably unrealistically) that perhaps we could establish a cloistered group in our midst to witness and support our existence in the Church and our commitment to its mission. I recalled how the Redemptorists were assisted in this way by the Redemptoristine nuns, a cloistered group that would further the order's spirit through prayer. Or, more practically, I thought about the Maryknoll Cloister, which exists to give the witness through prayer to sisters who minister in the mission fields of the world. Providentially, this approach was not to be. Something else was on the horizon: the house of prayer movement.

While visiting and lecturing in the United States, moral theologian Bernard Haring, CSSR, spent a good deal of time addressing groups of sisters. He emphasized that a renewal of the kind and quality of prayer life was imperative in a post-Vatican Church. Such a renewal would challenge us and ground the new way in which we were finding ourselves among the people of God. To bolster his idea, he promoted the formation of houses of prayer, where such study and experimentation could occur. This was also an important theme of his retreat with us, and, as a result, one of the first enactments of the subsequent chapter.

Father Haring's observations about the spirit of houses of prayer were significant and have perennial meaning. He had moved about the country and in other parts of the world addressing many religious congregations on this topic. In 1965, he introduced the idea of the house of prayer to the Leadership Conference of Women Religious (then the Conference of Major Superiors of Women). That group, in turn, asked whether a congregation would be willing to act as a clearinghouse for such proposals for houses of prayer and provide an opportunity for those interested to meet and further discuss their meaning and implementation. The Monroe IHM congregation agreed to take on this role. In 1968, preparing to establish houses of prayer, we sponsored a conference entitled "Contemplative Living in the Contemporary World." Over 150 women and men religious met for five stimulating days to examine this issue.

Because Trappist monk Thomas Merton had been writing on the interaction of action and contemplation in the world, and was busy addressing a variety of groups intent on making the Council a living reality in the United States, we wrote to see whether he could attend one of our meetings. Merton replied that while he would very much like to be present, he was sure his abbot would not allow it. However, he encouraged me to take my chances and write to the abbot anyway. The answer from Abbot Dom James was swift and clear, more than suggesting that apparently I had no idea of what the vocation of contemplative Trappist monks involved. Obviously, he implied, they could not be traipsing across the country on demand! Merton wrote to say that if he could not come to us, perhaps we could come to him?

And so it was that in October 1968, five IHM sisters and Brother David Steindl-Rast, a Benedictine monk active in the house of prayer movement, travelled to the monastery of the Trappestine nuns in the Redwood forest north of San Francisco. Merton was on his way to visit with contemplative groups in the East, but could spare us a few days.

As we arrived at the monastery in a large station wagon, a man wearing khakis and a stocking cap approached. He leaned into the driver's open window and asked, "Is this the gang from Monroe?" That was how we met this unforgettable prophet and teacher of prayer. For a long weekend that October, we enjoyed the company, stimulation, conversation and wit of this most extraordinary man as we reflected with him and the Trappistine nuns on what houses of prayer might "look like" and, most especially, what they might offer the post-Vatican Church. While we had many stimulating conversations about the *what* and *why* of houses of prayer, what stays with me even now is the image of this deeply contemplative human being, so full of life, snapping pictures with his camera, sitting on a stool in the evenings dressed in jeans and a khaki shirt, reading his poetry to us and enjoying a bottle of beer (Coors Lite). One of the IHM sisters in our small company was Sister Ann Chester. She would become a tireless traveller, promoting and studying the impact of houses of prayer among Catholic sisters as well as among lay women and men of various cultures and religions. Merton affectionately called her "the Apache," partly, I think, because of the colourful poncho she wore.

Merton left the Redwoods one day ahead of us. On our last morning together, he celebrated the liturgy and then participated in one more opportunity for sharing. He referred to his own quest and some of the uncertainty that surrounded it. The mood was different from that of the previous days. The rather mischievous and teasing monk seemed to have gone somewhere else, already looking ahead to his journey to Asia and what he would find there.

For some years, Merton had been studying and reflecting on Buddhism in its rich and various forms. He was particularly drawn to the abundant possibilities of Christian-Buddhist conversation. As well, he was growing more deeply attracted to life as a solitary hermit. Gethsemani had become too public, with too many visitors and curiosity seekers hoping for a glance at the famous author of *The Seven Storey Mountain* and of the strong and challenging essays on peace, justice and the civil rights movement. The abbot had agreed that when Merton returned from the East, he could locate to a more remote place of hermitage, even in another geographic area, all the while remaining attached to Gethsemani, which would always be his monastic home.

Brother Patrick Hart's foreword to *The Asian Journal of Thomas Merton* lays out the backdrop to this journey east, while Amiya Chakravarty, consulting editor, offers a reflection on what he calls Merton's Tibetan inspiration. Chakravarty notes that "the monk of Gethsemane did not desert his own indwelling heights when he climbed to meet the Dalai Lama in the Himalayan mountains. In a way his discipleship of Jesus grew as he gained the perspective."

Mary McDevitt, IHM, who was one of our group, remembered that Merton shared, on that last morning, some of the deep questions and uncertainties that lay ahead. He asked for our prayers. He seemed to be a searching man on a mission, but an interior mission to recognize the truthfulness of Buddhism. "Pray for me. I will face things I do not know." At the liturgy, he prayed, "Come, Lord Jesus. You are the Alpha and the Omega." His recitation of the Benedictus left us with new and deep insights, since we heard it through his searching mind and heart.

In our last sharing session, Merton asked each of us to reflect on a passage of scripture that was particularly meaningful and challenging for us. We did not get beyond his reflection, the first. Merton read from Romans 8:1. In this verse, he said, is the true meaning of Christian freedom: "The reason, therefore, why those who are in Christ Jesus are not condemned, is that the law of the spirit of life in Christ Jesus has set you free from the law of sin and death...."

Merton left for the East the next day. His journal notations as the plane took off express his feelings. "We left the ground—I with Christian mantras and a great sense of destiny, of being at last on my true way after years of waiting and wondering and fooling around ...."

Less than two months later, on December 10, Thomas Merton died from an electrical shock in Bangkok. His body was flown back to his Abbey of Gethsemani in Kentucky on an army plane, along with the bodies of young U.S. soldiers who had lost their lives in the Vietnam War. It was a paradoxical journey for this outspoken monk, who had written so powerfully for peace and so strongly against the evil of this war.

I wonder if he found what he was seeking there in the East and in the presence of the great stone Buddhas at Polonnaruwa. Here in part is what he wrote in his journal at the time:

> I am able to approach the Buddhas barefoot and undisturbed, my feet in wet grass, wet sand. Then the silence of the extraordinary faces. The great smiles. Huge and yet subtle. Filled with every possibility, questioning nothing, knowing everything, rejecting nothing ... Looking at these figures I was suddenly, almost forcibly jerked clean out of the habitual, half-tied vision of things, and an inner clearness, clarity, as if exploding from the rocks themselves became evident and obvious ... I don't know when in my life I have ever had such a sense of beauty and spiritual validity ... Surely with Mahabalipuram and Polonnaruwa my Asian pilgrimage has come clear and purified itself. I mean, I know and have seen what I was obscurely looking for. I don't know what else remains but I have now seen and have pierced through the surface and have got beyond the shadow and the disguise.[3]

On our return from our time with Merton in California, a group of eight sisters, under the leadership of Mary McDevitt, IHM, became the "founding community" of an IHM house of prayer. The community's purpose was to study and to bring the house of prayer experience into the reality of IHM life. Although many other religious communities began similar ventures in various locations, we took the concept up much more intentionally. An old but sturdy abandoned horse barn on the back property of the IHM mother house, used to store farm equipment, was turned into an extraordinarily beautiful place of prayer that we named "Visitation." The name reflected the passage in Luke in which two women, Mary and Elizabeth, come together to praise the liberating meaning and message for the world that they carry in their own lives. The founding sisters took up residence in an old farmhouse adjacent to the barn and set about living and reflecting on what life in a house of prayer might mean.

On November 10, 1970, the 125th birthday of the IHM congregation, Cardinal Dearden dedicated the barn-chapel of the house of prayer. Father Haring, who came over from Rome, was also present. "Visitation" was now a reality. In time, a small retreat house and two hermitages were added near the woods on the same property.

Father Haring's observations about houses of prayer had a significant effect on the life and reflection of the "founding community":

> The House of Prayer must be a completely new form of contemplative living or else it has no excuse for existence. It must not be a cloister in the traditional sense. It must be open to the Church and to the world, bringing faith to all the realities of life and bringing them [the realities of life] to the House of Prayer.[4]

In the early years of Visitation, Father Haring was a regular visitor. He often made his own retreat there. For him, this place had become an incarnation of what he dreamed houses of prayer would be.

The core group who lived at Visitation developed the prayer life for the community. The group did not in any dramatic way withdraw from the world. Rather, the group members explored through prayer and study what it might mean—for the Church but also for the whole of humankind—to be actively contemplative in a world of change and challenge. For this reason, a good part of the group's time was spent in study and reflection of movements and events in the world and in the Church that would affect not only their prayer but also the ministry of

Visitation. It is significant that within five years, sisters from Visitation had carried spiritual prayer ministry to Africa, Brazil, the Philippines and Puerto Rico. Moreover, they went as missionaries to Vietnam, India and Grenada. The study of current problems, prayer "over" the wounds of the world, concern over the disadvantaged, was made experiential.

It was especially in Africa that the house of prayer movement had a major influence. Sister Annette Boyle, IHM, worked tirelessly there for many years. Because the house of prayer sisters had also been formed as spiritual directors and were qualified to conduct 30-day retreats in the Ignatian tradition, they were able to answer the desires of many African religious communities for renewal in prayer.

In time, the house of prayer movement would lose its original meaning as a force for renewal in the Church and in congregations of women religious. I suspect that part of the reason was that community living itself had undergone a dramatic change. The postmodern world confronted us with new challenges to our life and our ministry. New historical forces shaped our spirituality. By the time Visitation celebrated 25 years of existence, it had ceased to be a house of prayer with a resident community and had become instead a spirituality centre. Still, its force and attraction as a place of prayer and solitude continued. A questionnaire sent to the congregation regarding the influence of Visitation reflects its importance as an image of the priority of prayer and spirituality among IHM sisters. The property on which Visitation exists is now for sale.

The house of prayer tradition, meanwhile, continued elsewhere.

On October 15, 2005, on the feast of St. Teresa of Avila, Visitation North was inaugurated in Bloomfield Hills, Michigan, a suburb of Detroit. It is located in Marian High School, a prestigious educational facility sponsored by the IHM Sisters. A wing of the building that once housed the more than 40 IHM sisters who composed the faculty has become home to another incarnation of the house of prayer. Its mission statement begins with an invitation:

> We IHM Sisters invite you to join us at Our Spirituality Center.
>
> We offer you an opportunity to pause in the whirlwind of life as you enjoy an experience of contemplative presence.
>
> We invite you to studies in spirituality and to listen to the depth of your own life and heart …

Interaction with Contemplatives

Through my experience with the house of prayer movement, I forged relationships with contemplative women from a variety of religious communities. These links have proved, in a profound way, to be among the most stimulating and satisfying of my life. As early as 1969, when I was general superior, I received a letter from Gertrude Wilkinson, a Redemptoristine sister. The letter invited me to take part in a meeting of contemplative nuns from various orders to explore how the renewal of Vatican II might be implemented in their lives. Gertrude was one of a core planning group drawn from various contemplative traditions by Constance Fitzgerald, a Carmelite from Baltimore. Constance herself had laboured tirelessly to make it possible for American Carmelites to meet together with the aim of establishing a federation through which they could pursue common desires for the renewal of their lives in the post-Vatican Church.

At Woodstock, Maryland, at the former theologate of the Maryland Province of Jesuits, I attended what I soon learned was the first meeting of contemplative nuns in the United States and Canada, and perhaps in the world. Representatives from various traditions—Carmelites, Poor Clares, Passionists, Redemptoristines, Trappistines, Dominicans, Precious Blood Sisters, Maryknoll Cloister Sisters, and several other small groups—came together to reflect on their common mission as contemplatives in the post-Vatican Church. The core planning group of nuns for this historic meeting included five sisters. They were joined by Carmelite Thomas Kilduff and Jesuits Thomas Clarke and George Wilson.

Numerous efforts by certain Carmelite communities to meet together for sharing and collaboration had been systematically stymied by some of the nuns themselves. Church officials in both the Sacred Congregation for Religious and the Carmelite Generalate had also expressed discomfort. I was invited to attend the Woodstock meeting because of the IHM commitment to the house of prayer movement. Plans for the meeting were well under way when a letter from Cardinal Carberry, who had been appointed head of a commission of three U.S. bishops to oversee the renewal of contemplative monasteries, arrived. The letter asked the nuns to refrain from participating in any meetings or gatherings until their renewal was complete. Those responsible for the planning reflected on the letter, noting perspicaciously that the Cardinal had *asked* them to refrain from participation rather than issuing a direct order. A letter went out to participants noting that, in light of the Cardinal's request, it would be understandable if some did not wish to attend, but that the meeting would proceed as planned.

Not only was the planning committee's decision to move forward with the meeting not taken in a rebellious spirit, but it also had the support of Cardinal Shehan of Baltimore. After receiving Cardinal Carberry's letter, Constance Fitzgerald had gone to see Cardinal Shehan. Shehan said that the meeting should go on and that he would support it in his archdiocese. Only very much later did Constance learn from Bishop Breitenbeck that, before the meeting started, the apostolic delegate had called Cardinal Shehan and asked why he was supporting such a gathering. Apparently, Cardinal Shehan told the delegate that the meeting *needed* to take place, that the nuns needed to work together, that he was supporting it, and that Rome should keep out of it. Cardinal Shehan, who was the celebrant at the first Mass of the meeting, never told the nuns that he had had to come to their defense. He simply put his trust in who they were as contemplatives and knew that only they could interpret their own charism in a most authentic way.

In all the years since that time, in my experience with contemplative renewal, particularly with Carmelites, I have been deeply impressed with the steady and serene spirit of those who entered seriously into the process. Even in extremely difficult situations with members of the hierarchy, with some of their male counterparts, and at times among themselves, these women stayed true to their mission.

I have often pondered how and why the struggles that active congregations of women religious have with renewal have so often been marked by controversy and opposition.

The meeting at Woodstock coincided with the publication of *Venite Seorsum* (August 15, 1969), a document issued by the Sacred Congregation for Religious concerning the renewal of contemplative life. In the minds of the nuns, the fact that the document was issued at this time was no coincidence. Rather, it was a carefully planned manoeuvre of the Congregation for Religious. A statement accompanying the document acknowledged the desire of a significant number of sisters to experiment with the meaning of enclosure and material separation. However, the Congregation for Religious insisted that in order to conduct such an experiment, the nuns would need to obtain a dispensation from vows and develop another form of religious life. The statement added, paradoxically, " ... we are confident that, in this same way [namely, by dispensation] what might be prompted by the Spirit of God in these times will thereby not be suppressed or lost."

As general superior of the IHM congregation, I was able to host and offer space in our academy at Monroe for the first leadership group of 30 women elected by the Woodstock participants to create the structure of what would become the Association of Contemplative Sisters. Not long afterwards, we hosted the summer prayer seminar, which brought together a number of contemplatives to share their hopes and desires as women with a common calling in the Church.

By this time, because of their meetings together, the contemplative nuns were strong enough in their resolve to go forward with their own renewal and to be public about it. As a result, in 1975, I was invited to address the Canon Law Society and lay out for the members the difficult situation of the contemplatives.

There at Woodstock, through the sharing of stories and interpretation of experience, these women "heard each other into speech." In time, this process led them to find their political voice as well—and, eventually, to learn that the two practices are, in essence, one. I would discover later that this same kind of experience of "finding one's voice" and "hearing one another into speech" would also mark the journey of active religious women in claiming who we are in the post-Vatican Church. By their remaining obedient and responsible to their charism as contemplative nuns, and knowing that such obedience would invite conflict from Church authorities, a new experience of God would be called forth.

I came across the concept of "hearing each other into speech" many years later, when I was living and teaching in Toronto. I often read it back into our experiences as women in the Church in the 1960s and '70s.

In *The Journey is Home*, Nelle Morton, a feminist theologian, tells a story about a group of women who had come together to tell their own stories.

> A woman started, hesitating and awkward, trying to put the pieces of her life together. Finally she said, "I hurt ... hurt all over." She touched herself in various places as if feeling for the hurt before she added, "but ... I don't know where to begin to cry." The woman talked on and on and her story took on fantastic coherence. When she reached a point of most excruciating pain no one

> moved. No one interrupted. Finally she finished. After a silence, she looked from one woman to another. "You heard me. You heard me all the way .... I have a strange feeling that you heard me before I started. You heard me to my own story."[5]

The women had heard her into speech and into the beginning of her healing. Perhaps our circumstances as women in the Church have not been as dramatic as the above story. Yet it is surely true that we have heard each other into speech.

Some spiritual writers and theologians claim that God is at times silent, hidden or withdrawn—*Deus absconditus*—and that in times of such silence we must wait patiently until God speaks again. "Perhaps," says Nelle Morton, "a more realistic alternative to such despair, or 'dark night of the soul,' would be to see God as the hearing one rather than the speaking one—hearing us to our own responsible word."

After "finding one's voice," a woman becomes more acutely aware of what it means to live in what theologian Rita Nakahshima Brock describes in *Journeys by Heart* as the "messy middle ... being conscious of how our circumstances, our loves, our fears, and our commitments enmesh us daily in ambiguous choices as we struggle to resist evil (violence) both within us and outside us."[6]

To resist evil and violence both within and outside us is to acknowledge ourselves as purposeful agents of salvation, and of responsibility, to ourselves and others, capable of moral discernment, courage, creativity and solidarity.

In the four decades that have passed since the historic meeting of contemplative sisters in Woodstock in 1969, they moved from silence to an initially awkward and faltering speech, and then to one of clarity and conviction. The process has been a characteristic mark of many contemplative monasteries of women who have sought to name and claim their experience within the Church and the world. Fidelity to that experience has borne much fruit in our efforts to make structural tensions life-giving and productive.

In many ways, this has also been our experience as women religious in apostolic congregations, as we have struggled to find our own voices in the Leadership Conference of Women Religious.

In some instances, contemplative women and men of the same religious family have ministered together. They have shared the gift of their charisms, not only with other religious women and men of active orders but also with the laity. This sharing has been and is a particularly creative way of actualizing the Council's insistence that all the people of God are called to the same holiness. Mindful that the charisms of religious orders and congregations do not exist only for their own members but also for the benefit of anyone who seeks a closer union with God, a group of Carmelites—women and men—founded what has become the Carmelite Forum. For the past 25 years, the forum has conducted seminars on the Carmelite classics at Saint Mary's College in Notre Dame, Indiana. Many women religious attend these seminars, as well as a significant and perhaps dominant number of lay women and men.

Deepening Discernment

As religious congregations of women and men faced the restructuring and renewing of their lives, the whole area of spirituality faced a major crisis and challenge. In a majority of active congregations of women religious, and certainly in my own IHM community, the measure of our spirituality had traditionally been how well we kept the rule and how generously and zealously we performed our teaching ministry. The spiritual exercises of each day were spelled out; we were expected to perform them every day without fail. Each summer during the annual retreat, the general superior would meet the whole community for the "reading of the rule." She would call our attention to areas in which we had failed, and would exhort us to greater fidelity and generosity. Many of us would jot those points in notebooks and from time to time, probably on the retreat Sunday at the beginning of each month, review them.

To be a truly prayerful religious did not so much mean growing in contemplative prayer or spending more time in prayer. Rather, it meant growing in virtue, which surely would happen if we kept the rule perfectly. We were not encouraged to read the mystics because, as active women religious, mysticism was not our calling. In fact, a desire for mystical experiences was discouraged as being "not our spirit." We were expected to be excellent and dedicated teachers, but were not to spend extra time at school, get overly engrossed with preparing for our classes, or get too close to the students. Although we were sisters who were "*in* the world," we were exhorted at the same time "not to be *of* it." A dilemma of major proportions was whether to be on time for the common visit to the Blessed Sacrament at 4:30 p.m. or to stay after school with a student who needed our special help at that time.

After the Vatican Council and in the early days of renewal, I had a conversation with a particularly insightful priest. He remarked to me that, in his opinion, women religious in active congregations had what he called "the worst of both worlds." Because we were sisters, we were to be with non-religious only to the degree that our duties demanded it. We were expected to return to the convent as soon as possible after teaching and not stay in our classrooms "wasting time" chatting with the students. But at the same time, any sister who seemed to take extra time in chapel on Saturday or after night prayers was looked upon with some suspicion. We were active sisters, after all—not contemplatives.

Before the time of the Vatican Council, IHM sisters did not have their own bibles, nor were they allowed to choose their own meditation books. Our only freedom in such matters was the possession of what we called "poverty books," small notebooks in which we could copy prayers of our choice and quotations from spiritual writers. This practice had come down to us from Theresa Duchemin, our co-founder, who felt that sisters should have some freedom with regard to their private devotions. In a poverty book, a sister could express her preferences in prayer, cultivate her own devotions and exercise some freedom of choice.

However, not every IHM sister liked the practice of having a poverty book. In an interview in 1993, a sister then in her 80s recalled with great amusement her own resistance to creating or using a poverty book as a book of prayer:

> I never had a poverty book because I never wanted one. I had an aversion to them. Early in my life, before I entered the community, I prayed the psalms. I wanted a book of psalms, nothing else. When the General Superior came for visitation to the mission where I was stationed, she said to me, "I hear you have no poverty book."
>
> I answered, "No, I do not—I have never had one."
>
> And then she said to me, "Everyone has a poverty book and I understand that you have your own book of psalms." She said that that was not our custom. "We can have a poverty book and a missal but nothing else. And so I want you to know that you have got to give up your book of psalms."
>
> And so I did and continued to read the psalms from the common bible in the community library. And to this day, I *still* read the psalms.

In those days, the superior chose our spiritual reading, and the mystics were not an option. Our spiritual formation was built on the stated premise of spiritual writers and teachers of prayer that there were two ways of reaching spiritual perfection: the ascetical way, that of acquiring virtue, or the mystical way. The latter was not within our reach and should be beyond our aspirations. Ours was the ascetical way. Books such as *The Spiritual Life* by Adolphe Tanquerey were standard texts.

The Ignatian Retrieval

In the mid- to late 1960s, the Canadian Jesuits of the English-speaking Province, in fidelity to the Council's call to religious orders to reinterpret the charisms of their founders in the light of the times, began to reclaim the charism of prayer so richly developed by St. Ignatius.

In Guelph, Ontario, at the Jesuit novitiate, Father John English, SJ, and some other Jesuits began to offer individually directed retreats of 30 days—not only to Jesuit novices and scholastics, but also to women religious, particularly those responsible for formation in their own congregations. The retreat was conducted in strict silence and followed the pattern of the spiritual exercises of St. Ignatius—a rich and powerful tool to lead participants to spiritual freedom and the ability to discern the movements of God within their spiritual journey in daily life. Each participant was to be personally directed. There were to be no public conferences. The retreat was to be followed by ten days of reflection on the experience, which included participation and sharing among the retreatants.

John English had been deeply influenced by Peter Paul Kennedy, SJ, a Jesuit at St. Beuno's Retreat House in Wales, where John English had made his long retreat before final vows. Rather than preach the 30-day retreat to a group of Jesuit tertians (those in the final stage of formation), which had become the custom, Kennedy directed each of them individually. This experience made a profound impression on English and put him in touch once again with the original intent of the spiritual exercises of St. Ignatius.

John English's influence back home in Canada was formidable. Ask any one of the sisters who went to Guelph in 1969, the first year that he and some other Jesuits offered the exercises to a number of women religious. Strongly committed to the rigour and purity of the exercises, he insisted on that same rigour in directing them and teaching others to do the same. Many IHM sisters went to Guelph in the late 1960s and 1970s for retreats. One IHM participant, having heard English state emphatically that the exercises would be conducted in absolute silence except on break days, publicly inquired whether silence was not "somewhat pre-Vatican." In his typical frank manner, and with each consonant punctuated, he replied, "There is nothing pre-Vatican about silence." Emphasis on *silence*, and end of inquiry!

Two or three years later, the two IHM sisters in charge of formation (sisters Lorraine Humphrey and Martha Rabaut) took the novices to Guelph. As he directed the young Jesuits, English taught the two sisters how to direct the exercises. When the first break day came, English noted with some dismay that these young novices, male and female, all seemed to know one another's names. How could this be? Were they not keeping the silence? The two IHM sisters were surprised at his lack of awareness. Where was he? At the kiss of peace at daily liturgy, when these young women and men moved across the aisle, they would greet one another, saying, "Hi, I'm Carole from Detroit." "Hi, I am Peter from Halifax."

I believe that the Ignatian revival of the exercises in this communal way at Guelph helped paved the way for the establishment of Jesuit retreat centres in the United States. While the original rigour may have lessened in some ways, at Guelph one will still find the original expectation of profound silence and deep reflection that permeates the atmosphere of retreats. In the late 1960s and 1970s, many members of women's congregations were deeply influenced, directly or indirectly, by the Ignatian movement and experience. Moreover, many entered more deeply into this ministry and became trained as spiritual directors themselves, which would have been unheard of in previous years. I think it is safe to say that male religious preached most, if not all, sisters' retreats prior to this time. A significant number of IHM sisters were given the opportunity to be trained in this way, and as a result were able to offer this same training to others.

By this time, the number of young women entering the congregation had diminished considerably. Moreover, in the changed context of our lives, formation itself posed a particular challenge for those entrusted with this ministry. The old way of formation was long gone. The novices no longer lived in the mother house but in a residence in Detroit. They were not to be formed according to the old formulas, nor was the IHM novice directress given the dire warning about "failing in her duty if she did not see to it that the novices would die to their own will and opinion." Thankfully, this approach was now nothing but a very bad relic of a former time.

As the next few years passed, a large number of IHM sisters made the long retreat and became excellent spiritual directors who could conduct the exercises. They offered workshops for members of other communities. IHM sisters also took part with Jesuits in giving retreats at other times and to other groups of religious. This was a rich and rewarding time. As our general chapter of 1972 approached, this richness had even more gifts to offer us.

A feminist critique of so much male-centred experience that had been normative for women as well as men made us conscious of this very real distortion. Our reflection on the spiritual exercises and their power would also have to undergo some critique in order to bring the richness of women's experience to bear on the exercises to deepen their value for us.

As a religious congregation, we had not been formed in the exercises. But a key aspect of the spirituality of St. Alphonsus Liguori, which imbued our founders, Louis Florent Gillet and Theresa Duchemin, was to enable others to learn to discern the love and presence of Jesus Christ in their lives. In this way, St. Alphonsus was like St. Ignatius. In fact, many in Alphonsus's time, when the Jesuits had been disbanded by the Pope, thought that Alphonsus was a Jesuit in disguise.

Discerning Together

The 1972 general chapter was a practical application of how the spiritual exercises influenced the IHM congregation in a key way. By this time, many sisters were making personally directed retreats, which enabled them to come to freedom and affirm their own persons in relationship to God, themselves and the world. This practice provided us with an important foundation at a time when so much was changing. Every sister in the community was invited to the 1972 chapter to take part in setting a direction for the future and articulating the affirmations that would define the meaning of our life together.

A deeply significant characteristic of this truly general chapter was the process of discernment and consensus that gave direction to all its deliberations. We were beginning to learn and to experience what discernment meant and what it required. We reflected on the belief that God speaks in our experience but that to discover that voice of God involves openness to deep listening and to naming false illusions as well as the true motivations for our actions. It was in this spirit that we engaged each other in all our deliberations.

Because we sensed the importance of this kind of spiritual freedom and responsibility, we stopped the chapter process for several weeks and asked as many sisters as possible to make a personally directed retreat over the Christmas holidays to get in touch with their deep desires and to confront, if necessary, the areas in which they were not free. We wrote to more than a hundred Jesuits to ask them to lead retreats; in the end, more than 30 accepted. They were joined by a number of our own sisters who were trained spiritual directors. The effects of the retreat process were positive: they reinforced our congregational desire to deliberate about our lives and ministries not through debate but through a process of discernment that would, we hoped, reflect the work of the Spirit in our midst.

I was to experience the power of such a process in a very graphic way from an unexpected source. Sister Callista was a woman in her early 90s whose mind was very sharp. She had decided views about the renewal of religious life and was unremittingly committed to wearing the habit. Each time I would address the mother house community, she would sit in the front row. Inevitably, she found an opportunity to publicly and loudly (she was a bit deaf) reprimand me for allowing any discussion about abandoning the habit. Such a decision, she strongly believed, would be in direct disobedience to the Holy Father's articulated wishes for us.

Sister Callista had committed herself to the chapter and, accordingly, made the first directed retreat of her life. I do not know who took on this intrepid woman in her prayer and discernment, but the outcome was a clear manifestation of their power. When the retreat ended, Sister Callista came to my office to announce that she was withdrawing from the chapter. She was peaceful, if still convinced of her commitment to the habit and our wearing of it. "I realized in my prayer," she said, "that I cannot give up my opinion about the habit and as a result I am not open, free enough, and therefore not able to discuss it."

The 1972 chapter was a rich experience that thoroughly engaged us. But as with all human endeavours, there were some shadowy and painful experiences when it came time to implement some of the chapter's affirmations.

The deliberations had provided for a representative assembly that, along with the officers of the congregation, was empowered to "shape the policies and structures needed to insure the proper implementation of the common expressions and desire of the congregation as a whole." The creative hope was that we might be able to keep alive, in a structural way, the rich process of prayer and discernment in which the chapter groups had functioned. Each member of the representative assembly (commonly called the RA) represented a group of sisters who met regularly to discuss ways to implement the affirmations of the chapter. Unclear and diverse concepts of authority and leadership surfaced again and again. As a result, the RA was ineffective and unable to function with ease and facility.

As part of the leadership team, I found this encounter to be very painful. I had already undergone several shifts in what my role meant in practice; some years later, I would be able to own the deepest source of my own discomfort with these painful exchanges. My concern was to safeguard what I perceived to be the role of leadership in the congregation. I had experienced the same painful conflicts when I was part of the Leadership Conference of Women Religious (see Part III), as we struggled with Rome over how we could and should be engaged in charting and implementing the renewal of our lives as women religious—only now I was on the side of authority.

In my official report to the congregation as my term of general superior came to a close in 1976, I submitted what I saw as a challenging question for future leaders. Rereading it many years later, I still believe that it has some relevance:

> Are we open enough, faith-filled enough, free enough and unfearful enough to confront and be confronted by the conviction that we are by solemn and public commitment a community gathered in the name of Jesus? That our deepest liberation from crippling oppression lies in the need of constant conversion and the searching of our own hearts for the truth about ourselves that really and only can set us free?

I recognized my own need to reflect on that question.

Women Theologians

In the late 1960s, as I began to attend many meetings of bishops and to interact with clerical persons in the Church, I had become more and more aware of the theological dependence of women religious on the views and expertise of clerics. In discussions on renewal, the Vatican documents or the life of the Church in general, we sisters were always reminded of our need to defer to male theologians and male teachers for the final word.

Sometime in 1968, while attending a meeting in Belgium after a trip to Rome, I had a conversation with Father Pierre Paré, a priest chaplain at the University of Louvain. I was remarking on our difficulties in conversations with Vatican officials in Rome. Each time we brought forward our opinions and convictions about renewal, which had come from our lived experience, we were told that we did not have the expertise to make these judgments and should leave them with the theologians—all male, of course—who were empowered to do the interpreting.

"Well," answered Father Paré, "why don't you educate your own theologians?"

On returning home, this idea stayed with me. It became clear to me that we would never be able to speak as peers in a hierarchical church until some of our women were as well educated as the male clerics and theologians. A dream began to take shape in my mind. What if we had one theologian for every hundred sisters in the congregation?

Perhaps then, I thought, we would be able to discuss matters as equals. As I explored this idea with my council, we decided to send ten sisters to pursue studies in various fields of theology and scripture, which would indeed give us one theologian for every hundred sisters. There was no condition imposed to say that they must come and teach in our college afterwards; they would simply use their education wherever it was needed. These ten women went to Louvain, Rome, the University of Notre Dame, the Catholic University of America, and other leading universities. All of them completed their degrees: an unusually high ratio. They obtained doctoral degrees in a range of areas of study—moral and systematic theology, spirituality, scripture, and canon law. In time, they taught in seminaries and on faculties of theology in the United States, Canada, South Africa and Rome. Having our own theologians also enabled us to conduct a theological program of high calibre for our own sisters. Over the years, IHM theologians, especially in summer sessions, did a good deal of ongoing theological education of IHM sisters and of the laity. Two of the ten sisters have since left the congregation, but they, like the other eight, continue to be forceful and influential theological educators and writers. As a result of this initiative, many other religious congregations across the country were inspired to send some of their sisters to study theology.

Today, the mood is changing again. As women begin to claim their own persons and their own opinions, many IHM sisters feel that there is no need for the so-called experts. Are we not all theologians in some sense? For me, an obvious acceptance and at the same time a disclaimer undergirds such an assumption.

Global Outreach

By the time I was elected general superior in 1966, the IHM congregation had long since extended its outreach beyond the United States. Our first mission outside the U.S. was to Puerto Rico in 1948. It was a ministry of education in schools, not unlike our primary work at home, though in very different circumstances. Our next mission reflected the swiftly changing culture into which we had moved.

Early in his pontificate, Pope John XXIII made an urgent plea to North American dioceses and religious congregations to send ten per cent of their priests and religious to Latin America. In response, in 1965 the IHM congregation, in conjunction with the Detroit Archdiocesan Mission, sent four sisters to Recife, Brazil, to work with two Detroit priests. This momentous decision reflected the tumultuous culture of the 1960s. Ministering under the leadership of Dom Helder Camara brought about a whole shift in a theology of mission, and led IHMs into the world of the emergent liberation theology of the Latin American bishops. Dom Helder was particularly close to his priests and to the sisters who ministered in his diocese. He would often visit them and take time to get to know them personally. He had an infectious and joyous personality.

Visiting Brazil six times during my years as general superior had profoundly broadened my perspective and my sense of global realities. This was my first experience of a bishop who was so strikingly simple, who when he spoke would hold both your hands and look directly into your eyes with clarity and with sincere affection. IHM sisters who went on missions in Brazil during the 40 years of our presence there developed a whole new consciousness. They lived in a socio-political context marked by years of military dictatorship and served a people who continually struggled to survive without the basic necessities of life. They also met a deeply spiritual people. As one IHM wrote, "We met people who had never made a retreat or read a spiritual book, but who were constantly aware of God's presence and had a profound union with God."

During the year of my presidency of the Leadership Conference of Women Religious (1972–1973), Dom Helder Camara addressed our national assembly in Washington, D.C.

In a 2005 publication of Leadership Conference occasional papers, I reflected on his visit.

That year was fraught with challenges arising from a series of explosive world events. The last phase of the Vietnam War was beginning. In Africa, war between the Hutus and the Tutsis raged on. The civil war in Cambodia was at its height. The Organization of Petroleum Exporting Countries (OPEC) was bargaining with the rich countries of the West, to the detriment of the poorer nations of the world. The United States was fast becoming a powerful empire, even as millions of Americans lived in desperate situations unworthy of the human condition. In Chile, the Pinochet coup initiated a reign of terror and oppression. Already, the Vatican was pulling back on the speed with which the Church was internalizing the reforms of Vatican II. The work of liberation theologians met with opposition; they were suspected of having Marxist leanings. Congregations of women religious felt the Church's disapproval of how we were implementing the Council's recommendations. Some congregations lost their status as canonical institutions.

Into this context entered Dom Helder Camara, a dynamic bishop barely five feet tall. At the 1973 Conference of Major Superiors of Women in Washington, DC, he challenged us as women leaders in our congregations to be among what he called "Abrahamic minorities"—that is, "persons, minorities determined to fight in a peace-filled, yet valid way for the formation of a more just and human world ... for today, as yesterday and always, determined, lucid, and courageous minorities were, are, and will be able to construct the world."

In a final and striking challenge he said,

> In the midst of the 600 Major Religious Superiors of the U.S.A., the Holy Spirit surely calls at least 60 to the option of trying to concretize the social encyclicals of the Popes, the documents of the Second Vatican Council and of Medellín, clear consequences of the Gospel. Sixty determined superiors will be able to move a great part of six hundred.

Nearly 40 years later, that call, in a new context, seems to me as relevant and challenging as ever.

One of the most rewarding phenomena of the 1970s was the wonderful global outreach of so many IHM sisters to the suffering of the world and to its urgent needs. Many IHM sisters took on these initiatives on their own, while other opportunities arose for leaders of congregations as they attended meetings of women religious and other groups.

Meeting Mother Teresa in Rome in 1971 led two IHM sisters to spend time working with the dying and caring for sick orphans, many of whom had been abandoned. Mother Teresa had made it clear to the gathered group of major superiors that she had attended this meeting for no other reason than to see whether she could recruit some sisters to come to India. She had no time for a discussion of the renewal of religious life in the face of the sorrow and struggle that many people were living amid famine and flood. That point in itself was a sobering thought and a wake-up call about our priorities. The famine in Bangladesh was in full force: Mother Teresa had to send some of her own sisters from the Home for the Dying in Calcutta to attend to the needs of the sick and dying in the neighbouring country. She was in search of sisters who could come to Calcutta, work in the home in place of some of her sisters, and perhaps do some teaching in the Home for the Dying.

Mother Teresa wanted more than vague promises. "Give me the names now! I must apply for permits and permissions," she told us. She would brook no delay. When we said that we would need to bring up this question "back home" and consult with our respective councils, she simply cut us off, repeating, "Give me the names now." I gave her the names! Afterwards, I moved aside as Sister Elizabeth (Betty) Carroll, RSM, approached. She said that after she returned home to Pittsburgh she would call her council and they would discuss this important issue. She received the same blunt response: "No—too late—give me the names now!" Betty looked over at me with an unspoken and incredulous question on her face: "What did *you* do?"

"Gave her the names," I replied with a resigned shrug.

Later, after the meeting, I chanced to meet Mother Teresa in the hallway. She was walking by herself. I approached her and asked somewhat boldly whether she would write down in a few words what religious life meant for her. I still have and cherish the small page torn from a notebook upon which she wrote in pencil on a cold November afternoon in a corridor of the Vatican:

> Religious Life is a life of surrender to Christ's call—without reserve it is a cleaving to Christ—and so to allow Him to live His life of Poverty, Obedience, Chastity, Charity. It is the life of the vine and the branch—and His Father the vinedresser. It is a life of undivided love.

> Accepting His Will—accepting Him in whatever form
> He may come.

More poignant still in those years was our work with orphans in Vietnam and refugees from Southeast Asia in camps in the United States. Having received a generous grant, I travelled to Vietnam with Sr. Lorraine Humphrey, an IHM who had ministered in Puerto Rico, and was at that time a provincial councillor. In Vietnam I saw first-hand the plight of the orphans. We visited many orphanages filled with thousands of babies and children, including children who had had polio. Many of these abandoned children had been fathered by American servicemen.

In Vietnam, two IHM sisters responded to these needs in a variety of ways. They established a simple Montessori School for toddlers, taught older children and worked with the staff. In 1975, with the fall of Saigon imminent, they were part of the famous Baby Lift. Other IHM sisters assisted with the care and education of refugees from Southeast Asia living in camps in the U.S. as they awaited settlement.

While attending the general assembly of the Leadership Conference of Women Religious in San Francisco in 1968, I heard an urgent request from Sister Mary Vincent, the general superior of the Daughters of Mary. Then the largest community of black women in Africa, they were known as the *Bannabikira*. Their greatest need was to be able to give their own sisters a high school education so they could obtain higher degrees and, in turn, educate their fellow sisters. The stirring words of Pope Paul VI echoed her request: "Basic education is the primary object of any plan of development, indeed starving for education is no less debasing than starving for food" (*Populorum Progressio* [On the Development of Peoples], no. 35).

Because IHM sisters were professionally formed as educators, and because English was the language in which they taught, a new field of missionary work opened out before us: first in Uganda in 1969, and later in Kenya, Ghana, Zimbabwe and South

Africa. In this work of extraordinary and zealous IHM sisters, the missionary spirit of St. Alphonsus Liguori came tangibly to life. Today, IHM sisters continue to minister in South Africa. They have had a remarkable influence through their ministry to people with HIV/AIDS.

One of my most inspirational moments in the African ministry of IHMs was a journey to Kenya, where I saw with my own eyes the courage and missionary zeal of the sisters. Sister Mary Jo Maher, the director of the IHM mission apostolate, had received a call from the U.S. State Department advising all U.S. citizens to leave Uganda as soon as possible. The "reign of terror" instigated by Idi Amin had begun. I travelled to Kenya with Mary Jo in 1973. We of course could not get into Uganda, and our missionaries could not easily leave. Under the pretext of shopping, they were allowed to go to Kenya; we met them in Nairobi near the airport. The conversation was a deeply moving one. The five IHM missionaries' decision to stay in Uganda was a sign of their deep commitment to the people they served. As the situation deteriorated, however, the sisters finally left. The last of them, who lived through harrowing experiences, was Sister Joan Mumaw. She stayed until June 1981, eight years after that momentous day of discernment. As of 2009, IHM sisters still minister in Uganda and South Africa, mostly in education.

Today, for many reasons, IHM's global outreach is diminished. The number of IHM sisters declined in the second half of the 20th century, and new forms of governance ordered the life of the community in different ways. The Detroit-Recife Archdiocesan Ministry ended, and the last IHM sister, Ann Nett, returned home after 25 years of commitment to the Church in Brazil. Our Overseas Province was dissolved in 1994 when the congregation adopted a new form of governance. IHM sisters who minister in Africa, Puerto Rico and Mexico no longer form a cohesive group. While these changes may have been part of necessary restructuring, they divided these women who shared a common endeavour in overseas missions.

However, in the words of Mary Jo Maher, the tireless co-ordinator of the missions for many years, "Reflection on the history of IHM overseas missions reveals that a compelling vision motivated individual missionaries and the missionaries as a corporate group to give without counting the cost. It is a gift of the Spirit that enriched the IHM congregation beyond measure."

The Messy Side of Renewal

The renewal of our lives, with all its promise, was not without its messy side. This "messiness" was revealed in countless ways, small and large—some of them rather laughable in retrospect.

By the late 1960s and early 1970s, the young women who entered the congregation not only asked new questions, but also reflected the general anti-establishment attitude of the day. Typically, for the times, they lacked respect for a number of time-honoured ways of doing things and wanted a voice in all that concerned them. They wanted to plan their own vow ceremonies. The days of walking up the main aisle in the mother house as a bride in a white dress and veil as the congregation sang "O virgin, happy bride" were long gone! By now, the congregation had formed into provinces. Many of the young professed sisters wanted to make their final vows in the parishes where they served, and to leave a mark of their own personalities on the ceremonies. Initially, this prospect sounded innocent enough but words cannot express the cumulative horror (at least in my opinion) that ensued!

The following examples illustrate not only the creativity and independence of these young women, but just as surely my own inability to adjust to the signs of *their* times. One young sister, who was charismatic, made her vows on the Feast of the Annunciation. She danced barefoot up the aisle wearing a long peasant skirt, preceded by another young woman carrying a banner that, as we saw when it was turned and placed in the sanctuary, bore one word in bold letters: Pregnant. (This referred, of course,

2340 Glynn Street, Detroit, Michigan, where all the Brennans grew up

The Brennan family circa 1929:
Back row: my mother (Ann), Richard, Mary Catherine
Middle row: my father (Henry), Martin (baby), Ellen, Ann, Henry Jr.
Front row: Margaret (me!)

The Brennan siblings in 1931: Martin, Ellen, Margaret, Henry, Ann, Richard, Mary Catherine ...

... and in 1967.

THE MOTHERHOUSE
Left wing, Novitiate; center, Chapel; right wing, Professed Sisters' quarters; the T wing, Infirmary

The IHM Mother House, Monroe, Michigan. Left wing, novitiate; centre, Chapel; right wing, Professed Sisters' quarters; the T wing, Infirmary

Visiting Day with my sisters: Mary Catherine, me, Ann, and Ellen, St. Joseph's Lake (by the mother house), Spring 1948

Margaret in 1973

With Lorraine Humphrey, IHM,
on our trip to Vietnam in 1975
to see how we could help with orphans there.

With Dom Helder Camara, Archbishop of Recife, Brazil, in 1972

With Bishop Kenneth Untener in 1992

With Thomas Berry, CP, in Toronto in 1993

With Joan Chittister at our "Elephants" meeting in Detroit, when Joan was the major speaker in 2006

Margaret at 84

to Mary and her "yes" at the Annunciation, but in the midst of the rubrics of the ceremony, I wondered if the message really carried over.) After she made her vows, we were all invited to pray over her (in tongues, if we were so gifted) as she knelt in the main aisle. I remember hissing as quietly as I could into the ear of the provincial superior, whom I had accompanied to the ceremony, "We're not going anywhere!"

Another very creative young sister who ministered in the deep South led a jazz quartet down the aisle, singing, "Oh a hap, hap, hap, hap, happy day. Oh a happy day." The congregation was invited to throw pumpkin seeds to accompany the outgoing procession, though I could never figure out why. As *Jesus Christ Superstar* was the musical of the year, almost no profession or reception could take place without listening to the hit song "I Don't Know How to Love Him," sung in the show by the Mary Magdalene character. This was often particularly puzzling to the parishioners and the families of the young sisters, who exchanged confused glances as this biblical heroine sang of her relationship with Jesus: "And I've had so many men before in very many ways/He's just one more."

The critical attitude that gripped the country and that was shared by many in our community soon began to affect our own attitudes towards the directions in which the community would go. This situation became abundantly clear when, on May 1, 1974, in the name of the leadership team, I wrote what was later called "The Meat Letter." The letter cited how the media had been highlighting the famines and hunger that were plaguing the drought lands of Africa, and pointed out that nutritionists and economists were urging us as a nation to eat less beef as a way to conserve the grain supply. Moreover, at the Representative Assembly in early 1974, one delegate after another had noted that as a community we were searching and struggling for ways to simplify our own lives—to spare as to share. While our eating less meat might be only a small gesture towards giving relief to the starving millions, it was our hope that the publicized example of our committed concern might give the impulse to others.

Consequently, I suggested in the letter along with the Provincials that in 1974–75, from Pentecost to Pentecost, we challenge ourselves to have four meatless days a week. What we could save by such a sacrifice could be sent to the Catholic Relief Service to purchase grain for our needy sisters and brothers in countries struggling with famine.

The reaction to this letter was swift and abundantly clear. Many said that the leadership team had no right to tell them what to eat or not to eat. This was a matter of personal conscience, they said. It was then that I knew that the time when a general superior could expect an immediate and whole-hearted response to such requests had ended. The days of "Mother said" were over!

Many such things had come to an end in the world of the IHM Sisters. The seemingly interminable council meetings during those early months and years were filled with what I now call the "trauma of the trivia," as we began to live without the structures and strictures of the past. Local superiors came to monthly meetings bristling with questions that demanded answers. Things were getting out of hand, they claimed. More directives were needed. If the modified habit called for a *round* collar, what shall we say about those who are beginning to wear *pointed* collars? Did we know that some sisters were wearing *blue* blouses instead of *white*? That some sisters were departing altogether from the prescribed renewal concept and designing suits of their own, that sisters were seen on the Marygrove College campus eating ice cream bought at the Dairy Queen down the street?

At one council meeting, I recall us waiting anxiously as the first assistant phoned a Detroit convent in an attempt to dispel the report that the local superior had come to breakfast on a Saturday morning in her robe with curlers in her hair. Alas, the report was true!

We laugh now when we remember that such trivia troubled and even traumatized some of us. Yet it was a necessary and inevitable part of the passage to the real and deeper meaning and consequences to which the adaptation of religious life called us.

In 1967, two years after the close of the Second Vatican Council, Edward Schillebeeckx had written these prophetic words in *Vatican II: The Real Achievement*:

> The adaptation of religious life must be, first and foremost, a re-evangelizing of all its structures. The consequences of this conciliar maxim are more numerous than a superficial reading of it would seem to indicate. The text gives the Church an inspiration whose charismatic consequences, I feel, cannot even be surmised at this moment. But eventually this 'supreme rule' will break through, without any clashes, we trust, though some will occur.[7]

The charismatic consequences of the re-evangelizing of religious life did break through and the clashes occurred as well.

In 1969, when the congregation had prepared for the special renewal chapter prescribed by Pope Paul VI in his letter *Ecclesiae Sanctae*, we had more deeply internalized the meaning and implications of the Vatican documents for religious life and had begun to interpret them in light of other documents, notably *Gaudium et spes* (*The Church in the Modern World*), *Ad gentes* (*The Decree on Missionary Activity*) and *Dignitatis Humanae* (*Declaration on Religious Freedom*).

This Renewal Chapter marked a significant change in our self-understanding. It became clearer that our concept of religious life was irrevocably marked by new and fundamental directions:

- a shift of accent in prayer, which did not denigrate its contemplative stance but sought rather to discover God in the human experiences of life;

- the search for the articulation of an apostolic spirituality that recognized human experience as a locus of God's ongoing revelation;
- a move from religious life seen essentially as a personal consecration to include prophecy, witness and *diakonia*;
- a less passive acquiescence to obedience and monarchical hierarchical structures;
- a move away from monastic forms of religious life and sacral symbols (religious habits, titles and names);
- a feel for history, evolution, and non-static world views, which relativized the note of permanency inherent in the traditional concept of the vows;
- an emphasis on concepts of mutuality, participation, collegiality, subsidiarity and the servant role of authority;
- a conviction that constitutions were to be primarily inspirational and visionary rather than prescriptive and cautionary; and
- a belief that law was to provide for the rights of the individual.

In general, the liberal view of Vatican II saw the Church moving from a focus on the sacral, corporate stance of religious institutions to a focus on mission, together with an accent on personal dignity, responsibility and human fulfillment, especially through the interpersonal lives of the unique individuals called to celibate commitment in community.

Yet, in spite of all the positive movements forward, the years of the late 1960s and early 1970s were ones of turmoil for both religious congregations and the Church hierarchy. A mixture of both negative and positive elements impinged on the renewal of religious life. Challenge and confusion prevailed as we internalized the concepts that the Council initiated.

The congregation struggled with new forms of government, provincial boundaries and membership. Difficult periods of discerning accompanied the movement into new ministries: what was a Church ministry and what was not? Perhaps most painful was the departure of so many of our sisters and friends into other ways of life. How we dreaded at the end of each year the long lists of the names of those who had left! For me, speaking with more than 300 sisters who were struggling with their own calling brought me to the realization that God's will was not a blueprint drawn up for all eternity, but a dynamic living force whose meaning we must continually seek in the depths of our hearts.

This insight brought about a major shift in my thinking about the whole theology of vocation with which I had grown up. It had been standard teaching that there was no such thing as a temporary vocation. Once given by God, the grace of vocation was irrevocable. If one left, it meant that one had never had a vocation in the first place, or one had ceased to pray and therefore had lost the vocation. As I spoke with those who were leaving, I discovered in the depths of my mind and heart that there was something wrong with such a teaching on vocation. These women had not stopped praying, and I had no guarantee that they were not called in the first place. In the light of the Council documents, with their strong call to the laity to carry out the mission of the Church, I sensed that a vocation to religious life had a different dimension to it. Whether they were younger or older, many of these women who were leaving religious life had realized that they were called not to consecrated life as a religious, but to work as lay persons in the Church. Exactly what is the call of religious today is something that needs a great deal of our prayer and reflection.

Watching the novitiate shrink from 60, 70 or 80 to 20, 15 or 10 filled those of us who remained with numbing fear as we looked to the future. During my fourteen years in formation as assistant and as novice directress, I had lived my life in the wing of the mother house that was home to postulants and novices.

Even as I write, I can touch the deep feelings of incredible sadness and loss for something "that was there for me once" as I walked by myself through the empty rooms on the evening of the day that the novices moved away into a whole new way of formation.

III

Brushwork

1

Leadership Conference of Women Religious

As I noted previously, in the journey of women religious in the United States, we have discovered our own voices as women and heard each other into speech. Because of our one baptism into the Risen Christ, in whom there is no distinction of gender or race, many of us, as women and as women religious, hold out hope for and lay claim to a place and a voice in the Church as full participants in its life and mission. Such a claim involves a journey of light and shadow—some moments are brilliant and shining, while others are muted and mottled by shadows. The shadows produce a lesser light, but paradoxically, the light is not necessarily less lovely.

It is more than an interesting aside to recall that this same metaphor of light and shadow was used in the *Lineamenta*. This document prepared by the Vatican in 1993 described the relationship of the U.S. bishops and American women religious in view of the upcoming Synod on Religious Life in 1994.

The metaphor of light and shadow reminds me of beauty honoured among the Japanese that stemmed from a simple reality of life. Forced to live in dark rooms, an older generation that did not have access to electricity in their homes and other buildings came to discover beauty in shadows.[8] Ultimately, they harnessed shadows to add to the beauty of a place. For many years, Japanese architects and builders have employed this deep psychic phenomenon when designing homes and gardens, shrines and temples, and even places of business.

The Conference of Major Superiors of Women first came into being in a reflected light. This organization sprang, surprisingly enough, from the Vatican. In the aftermath of the Second World War, Pope Pius XII was convinced of the power of women and men religious to become catalysts for healing and transforming the so-called Christian West, which had been devastated by two brutal wars and the horror of the Holocaust. He hoped that collaboration among religious and their shedding of the outmoded customs and rules that they lived by would enable them to take on this role. As Archbishop Arcadio Larraona—Secretary General of the Sacred Congregation for Religious, and friend and confidant of the Pope—put it, the aim for religious was "to live in our times according to the needs of our times."[9]

The Vatican had encouraged the formation of national conferences of religious to foster ministry. In the end, this urging nudged the somewhat reluctant mothers general of the United States into making a beginning on November 24, 1956.

The women religious who had attended the first U.S. Congress of Religious Orders, held at the University of Notre Dame in August 1952, showed that as women they would become a force to reckon with. A column in the August 25, 1952, issue of *Time* magazine, under the heading "Religious and American," offered an inkling of what was to come.

> Before one of the sisters' discussion sessions, it was discovered that a priest was to address them on the subject of modern comforts and conveniences. Up rose a seven-member nun's committee to protest. Said Mother Mary Gerald O.P., the chairperson of the committee, "Why should any man tell us about our comforts and

> conveniences?" Four nuns were hastily scheduled to speak in the priest's place.
>
> "Simon-pure American," noted the reporter.
>
> The national committee of seven religious superiors from six different congregations who had been appointed by Rome to discuss the possibilities of a woman's conference first met in 1952. Their initial reflection was that such a further organization would neither be necessary nor beneficial. These women represented congregations of hundreds of sisters. They were aware that organizations such as the National Catholic Education Association, the Catholic Health Association, and the National Catholic Welfare Conference already allowed for fruitful collaboration in the fostering of a massive educational system, social agencies, hospital and health-care facilities.[10]

Nevertheless, even though these flourishing apostolates were sponsored and fostered by congregations of women, many of us can recall how these same congregations operated in splendid isolation from one another—ordering our lives, cherishing our own traditions, having our own colour and cut for our habits, following our own customs and our own spiritual practices. A little intramural comparison and competition about which of us were the most observant, the most dedicated, the most truly religious, emphasized our different approaches.

In 1956, the newly formed Conference of Major Superiors of Women was governed by an executive board representing regions of the country, similar to those regions of the National Catholic Education Association. The board members were entrusted with electing the officers and writing the statutes. Early assemblies dealt with questions of formation, the education of novice directresses and the spiritual lives of the sisters. The theme of the first regional program, in 1958, gives some indication of the preoccupations among women religious. With the Second Vatican Council a mere four years away, the program's focus was "Revitalizing Religious Life for the Individual and the Community Through Combating the Effects of Naturalism, Lack of Mortification, and Excessive Activity."

From the early 1950s, the sister formation movement, through the National Catholic Education Association, had drawn together women educators from diverse congregations to seek the advancement of the religious, cultural and professional formation of sisters. Through conferences, educational programs and, perhaps most especially, the widely read *Sister Formation Bulletin*, countless women religious in their convent residences in the United States read and discussed articles by new theologians.

Already, significant shifts in American culture and in other parts of the world were having a major impact on our lives. And then, in 1962, six years after the founding of the Conference of Major Superiors of Women, the Vatican Council swept over our lives like a giant tidal wave. The landscape of religious life was forever changed: the Conference was virtually refounded in the light of the Council. Mary Luke Tobin, a Loretto sister who was president at the time, had been invited to be an official observer at the Vatican. This request was a major breakthrough, since no women had been invited originally to be participant observers. Her influence in Rome, where she had input into the content of *Gaudium et Spes (The Church in the Modern World)*, was significant. Her activity as a true ambassador for the Council was unparalleled. She crisscrossed the United States giving talks and workshops on how religious life could and should reflect the Council's challenging and hopeful message and mandate.

A powerful tool in articulating the emerging thinking of women religious in the light of the Council was the Sister's Survey (1966–68). This questionnaire of some 645 items covered topics as diverse as one's concept of God, American participation in the Vietnam War, and the living and understanding of our vows. The results of the survey showed that not only was the world view of the lives of women religious being transformed, but also that religious life itself was going through unprecedented change. The research director, Marie Augusta Neal, a Notre

Dame de Namur sister, shared the survey's findings with major superiors at the Conference of Major Superiors of Women assemblies in 1967 and 1968, barely two years after the Vatican Council.[11]

All of this ferment had a deep effect on the Conference. In many ways, it was a season of high noon and high energy. This luminous time under a seemingly cloudless sky continues to influence and direct the life of the organization in its journey to today. Many of the major superiors at that time had been associated with the work of the sister formation movement. Because membership in the Conference was limited to major superiors, it was small but effective. Terms of office were longer than usual, allowing members to form deep bonds in the common challenge of the renewal that had been mandated by the Church. Indeed, we became a primary support group for each other. Often buffeted on the one side by resistant members of our own congregations and, on the other, by the bishops and the Vatican, we were able to strengthen each other at critical times. I felt such strength in community and solidarity personally in the years that I was active in the organization.

Back home, many of us were dealing with upheaval in our congregations. Some members confronted us with our supposed disobedience to the Pope. They felt justified in questioning or opposing the proposed changes to the congregation, even if these were chapter enactments and therefore voted on by the community. Gathering together at general assemblies, regional meetings or executive board sessions of the Conference of Major Superiors of Women was an opportunity for us to speak about these difficulties.

In our conversations with bishops and Vatican officials, we were not confrontational but we stood firm. We did not take the stands we did just to be stubborn. Increasingly, what Rome was telling us did not match what our experience was telling us.

In 1971, we completed a serious study of our bylaws over many months. During this process, which included all members of the Conference, we rewrote our bylaws with the aid of a group of consultants. We did so in the belief that the Conference was an expression of who we were as major superiors, fully intending to send the bylaws on to the appropriate Vatican officials in Rome for approval when the task was complete. We also changed the name of the organization to the Leadership Conference of Women Religious.

Rome opposed both moves. It would be more than ten years before the new statutes were finally approved, in 1988–89, and even then the new name was recognized only reluctantly. Using the term *leadership* and calling ourselves leaders was looked upon as an arrogant claim. Moreover, it reminded many Italian Vatican officials of Mussolini, who called himself "Il Duce," the Leader. Nevertheless, the strong sense of solidarity that we felt enabled us to stand together and offer articulate support when one congregation met with what we considered an abuse of power. This was especially true when we had quasi-official visits from members of the Sacred Congregation in Religious who felt that we were not renewing our congregations in the light of the Council but had gone beyond it. (That was probably true, to a certain extent.)

Officials at the Vatican likely would have preferred to deal with us one by one, but we did not want that to happen. We chose to stand together. Between 1968 and 1971, women religious in the United States faced a number of difficult crises. Both the Immaculate Heart of Mary Sisters in Los Angeles and the Glenmary Sisters in Cincinnati had major conflicts with their respective bishops regarding the implementation of their renewal. Because these same bishops appealed to Rome, both congregations were pressured either to comply or to become non-canonical groups. Both chose to stand firm, and lost their canonical status.

A particularly tense meeting of the Conference in St. Louis, Missouri, in 1969 was a harbinger of the struggle that many religious congregations would face in subsequent years. Cardinal Antoniutti, the Prefect of the Sacred Congregation for Religious, had sent a letter the previous year to all religious congregations instructing them that they could make no changes to their constitutions or way of life without the Vatican's permission. The letter further articulated what were called the essential elements of the renewal process, including wearing the habit and living the common life in established houses or convents. The IHM Sisters in California had already been publicly censured by Cardinal McIntyre for the changes they had made in this regard; he appealed to Rome for support. By this time, a number of major superiors in the country felt that the Conference should publicly express support for the California congregation, because many congregations were implementing similar changes.

The matter was debated by conference members not so much because of its content, but rather as to whether it showed disloyalty to the Church and its officials who had responded negatively to such a show of support. Father Edward Heston, a representative of the Congregation for Religious who was present at the meeting, told the major superiors in so many words that they should not pass any resolution regarding support of the California community. In general, the Conference response to Father Heston's admonition was swift and overwhelmingly negative. A lively debate ensued as superior after superior went to the microphone to speak in defense of the renewal to which we felt the Vatican Council had called us, and to support the California IHM Sisters.

The voices of Elizabeth Carroll, RSM, and Angelita Myerscough, ASC, officials of the Conference, were particularly strong. In some instances, the replies, accompanied by strong and strident arguments, verged on anger. A number of major superiors were shocked and offended by the manner in which some of the women spoke. The meeting ended in disarray, and the liturgy that followed was anything but a joyful experience of solidarity. Some participants even commented publicly that we should not be celebrating a liturgy in such an atmosphere of division. I believe that it is true to say that the seeds of a parallel leadership group, the Consortium Perfectae Caritatis, were planted that day.

Later, some attempts were made to avert the crisis of the IHMs in California, which had a Spanish foundation. (The California IHMs have no relationship to the Monroe, Scranton and Westchester [Pennsylvania] IHM congregations. Though separate from one another, the latter three have the same founder.) At first, a plan was made that a number of major superiors would travel to Rome with Anita Caspary, the general superior of the California IHMs, in the hope of speaking with Vatican officials. Bishop Joseph Breitenbeck was influential and helpful in inaugurating this plan. Ultimately, it did not materialize: instead, Rome organized a committee of bishops to study the case. Although talks and meetings went on, nothing really came of them. In time, the California IHM congregation split into two groups: one canonical and one not. Both groups are still active today. In 2003, Anita Caspary published a full account of this sad conclusion in her book *Witness to Integrity*.[12]

In the midst of life in the post-Vatican world and Church, we discovered that the winds of change also brought clouds and storms. There would be times and seasons when we experienced more shadow than light. The sea changes, in the Church and in the Conference, were both transformative and troubling. Was Jesus in our boat? We thought so, even if it seemed as if he were sleeping!

We were discovering as well that diverse views of renewal based on differing ecclesiologies in the documents of Vatican II were operative in our own congregation. This situation brought pain and internal division to individuals within communities and between communities.

And perhaps, very importantly, we were experiencing—though not yet able to clearly articulate—the place of culture: our own American experience as women religious in the Church.

2

The Consortium Perfectae Caritatis

In 1970–71, a group of major superiors who felt that the Leadership Conference of Women Religious had departed from the real meaning of renewal formed a new association, the Consortium Perfectae Caritatis. This move reflected deep tension about renewal of religious life in both Rome and the United States, and highlighted the irreconcilable differences that were surfacing among religious congregations. I believe it was the hope of the Consortium that it might officially succeed the Conference, if the Vatican approved. Many bishops were divided in their allegiance. In time, the Sacred Congregation for Religious joined the controversy as it tried to bring the two groups together.

My first encounter with this kind of ideological and theological difference among major superiors had occurred as we attended meetings together in our own local Conference regions. As we discussed *Perfectae Caritatis*, the Vatican's decree on religious life, and quoted from highlighted passages, it became clear that the document contained differing ecclesiologies. From them, one could argue two theologies of religious life. This, I noted later, was true of other documents of Vatican II as well.

I was president of the Conference in 1972–73. As president, I felt deeply committed to attempting to heal the breach between the Conference, which was supported by many congregations, and the Consortium, which was supported by a significant number of bishops. I visited the general superiors of several of the Consortium's founding congregations. They were courteous and receptive, but the division never really disappeared. At one point, some years after my presidency, representatives of both groups were summoned to Rome to discuss their differences with members of the Sacred Congregation for Religious, in the hope that some kind of reconciliation could be achieved. Six members of the Consortium and six members of the Conference, including me, sat side by side facing the Vatican officials, who sat at a long table covered with a red felt cloth. The table was placed on a kind of stage, over which hung the portraits of previous Congregation officials. The conversation was pleasant. I thought at the time that there was a real attempt to listen objectively to both groups, although I sensed that there was more genuine support for the Consortium.

A particularly poignant circumstance for me was that Sister Claudia Honsberger, the general superior of the IHM congregation from Westchester, was a staunch, influential and outspoken member of the Consortium. At one of the coffee breaks, I asked her a question: "Do you think [our co-founder] Father Gillet is having a bit of beatific schizophrenia as he looks down on us? Here we are with the same founder, the same spirituality, the same commitment to education, and at the same time are at opposite poles in our views of renewal!" We both had the grace to laugh.

My major problem with the Consortium was that I believed it compromised what we all were trying to do in relation to our own congregations. All of us had struggles in our own communities, trying to bring harmony to the many viewpoints about the renewal process. I thought it close to scandalous that we, as leaders of religious congregations of sisters, could not work out this issue. If we could not do so as a group, then how could we expect to do so within our own communities?

IHM congregations have changed considerably since those days. For better or for worse, what the leaders of communities do or say isn't all that significant. It occurs to me that in the early years of renewal, our actions had a lot more impact both for the Church and for the general public. I am not certain why this is no longer true; I suspect that it has much to do with the cultural shift congregations have undergone. However, it did matter in those days, because we were still emerging from hierarchical models, and what the mother general did was very important. As a result, it was painful for me when some women in my own congregation felt that our renewal was contrary to what Rome and the Holy Father were saying, and did not hesitate to make their opinions known.

Nevertheless, it was essential for us to be able to deal with differences. When the split in views led to the formation of the Consortium Perfectae Caritatis, confusion was the result. Many women religious began to see each other in terms of who was perceived to be loyal to the Pope and who was not. I thought that if we within the Conference could just keep talking with one another, perhaps things would change. I attended several Consortium meetings with the hope of further dialogue, but no such conversation occurred.

The Consortium had its own theologians. One of them was John Hardon, a dedicated Jesuit educator who had taught on the IHM Monroe campus in the summers for some years prior to the Council. Since I had returned from my theology studies as a relatively young sister, I had been involved in planning the summer theology programs. I had worked with Father Hardon over several summers. Initially, he found us to be a most rigid group of religious, incapable of the kind of flexibility that could make way for an interpretation of the rule that would favour its real purpose and the meaning of our lives as apostolic women religious and educators. At the time, I found his position offensive. My refusal to discuss the content of the summer classes after congregational night prayers, which would violate the unbreakable solemn silence, was incomprehensible to him. He asked to see the rule. Hoping to find some insight into our spirit, he looked, naturally, to the chapter on charity. There he found the metaphor used to describe the love that should exist among us: "Charity is the cement that holds the sisters together."

"Cement," he said incredulously. "That explains it all."

As the Vatican Council approached, I was beginning to internalize some momentous changes. When I became general superior and we were implementing the outcomes of Council, I received a letter from Father Hardon. For some reason, this formerly forward-looking Jesuit saw our interpretation of renewal as a misreading of the Council documents, and as detrimental to the Church. I lamented and sometimes fearfully pondered his words in the letter, which I kept for some years: "I gravely and sadly fear for your immortal soul." His association with the Consortium disappointed and disturbed me, because I knew so well the power and strength of his convictions.

Those religious congregations that came together under the Consortium obviously had some major concerns about renewal. Those of us in LCWR also wondered, "Were the directions of the Conference an authentic expression of religious renewal, or were they pointing to an understanding of religious life that was itself developing?" The Consortium's disapproval of our alacrity and enthusiasm in taking up the Council's directives left us shocked and initially incredulous.

The response of the Sacred Congregation for Religious to the renewal directions of many congregations—regarding the wearing of the habit; new forms of ministry, particularly in areas of peace and justice; and the adaptation of the way of life to be more suited to these new initiatives—was negative. The Congregation appeared to promote a static and stratified view of religious life, one we considered to be apart from the flow of history.

The ideals of the Consortium live now in the Council of Major Superiors of Women Religious, which received papal approbation in 1992. This brought to two the number of conferences of women religious in the United States.

In retrospect, I do not think I ever found anything positive in the Consortium struggle. Sometimes, in such ideological disagreements, it is possible to see difficulties as creative or to note that something life-giving comes out of them. I never had that insight. Yet, as one who spent many days and hours in the early years of Conference with the women who founded the Consortium, I still cherish the hope that one day we will be one Conference again, reverencing our diversity and giving witness to its fruitfulness as we minister together in the Church that we all love and serve.

3

Close Encounters with the Hierarchy

A poem of Emily Dickinson's describes well what happens when a deeply held perception is shattered.

It dropped so low—in my Regard—
I heard it hit the Ground—
And go to pieces on the Stones
At the bottom of my Mind—[13]

Perhaps these words are too strong, yet they express the pain and shock of a shattered perception, a dashed hope that the Church, in fulfilling its commitment to renewal, would call forth our gifts and our experience as women in ministry to meet new challenges. Instead, we came to the painful realization that Rome for the most part wanted to control us, and that our work with many in the hierarchy would be marked by struggle, our experience would be discounted, and we would face spoken and sometimes silent disapproval of who we were and who we had become in our desire to serve the Church.

It would probably be true to say that my encounters with bishops and the Roman hierarchy during the years I was active in the Conference contributed to many of my growing feminist convictions, though I did not name them as such at the time.

When I was president of the Conference, I cherished the hope that after our yearly meeting with officials of the Sacred Congregation for Religious we might be given an audience with the Holy Father to receive a blessing for the Conference as we came together at our national assembly. The request for such an audience was not intended to begin a dialogue or raise our concerns; rather, as leaders of congregations of women religious, we wished to be able to express our commitment to the Church. In the name of the Conference, I wrote to the Cardinal Secretary of State asking if we could bring greetings from the Conference to the Pope and receive his blessing.

For some time, we had no reply. Some weeks later, just as I was on my way to visit the IHM sisters in Brazil, I received a call from Father (later Bishop) James Rausch, who was secretary to Cardinal Krol. (Cardinal Krol of Philadelphia was the president of the National Conference of Catholic Bishops and a strong supporter of and advocate for the Consortium.) Father Rausch was calling to read me a letter that had been sent from the Vatican to Cardinal Krol. Cardinal Krol had instructed him to read it to me, since it was addressed to me as president of the Conference. The letter said that requesting a visit with the Pope was not advisable at this time.

I recall asking Father Rausch why the response had come across the Cardinal's desk rather than directly to our offices, since we wrote the letter ourselves and had addressed it directly to the Holy Father through the Cardinal Secretary of State and not through the National Conference of Catholic Bishops. Receiving no immediate answer, I risked a further question: "Was it perhaps," I asked, "because Rome had written first to Cardinal Krol as president of the bishops' conference to ascertain whether he thought it would be a wise thing to grant an audience in light of the problems with the Consortium?" Father Rausch did not answer. We were never given a copy of the letter, even after asking for it.

I felt strongly that as a Conference we had a right to know the truth. I called Cardinal Krol as I was leaving for the airport. He was in a meeting, but at my insistence came to the phone. I repeated what I thought had happened and asked what "a requested audience not advisable at this time" meant. The Cardinal's voice was tinged with impatience at what I presumed he saw as an impertinent request: "Well, Sister, when you clean up your own house, you might be acceptable to approach the Holy Father."

Shaken by his reply, I responded after a moment, "Your Eminence, *if* the Pope is the Vicar of Christ, then it seems to me that the people who have the greatest claim on his attention would be those who do *not* have their act together." To his irritating response, "Aren't you being a bit emotional?" I could only concur.

A few weeks later, on the eve of our national assembly in Washington D.C., we received a communication from Archbishop Jean Jadot, the apostolic delegate. He notified us that he had a letter in the Vatican pouch with more explicit information regarding the refusal of the papal audience. The tenor of the response was that the Conference and its membership were not following the channels under which the Pope normally dealt with women religious. Consequently, until we were able to work out that process, it would not be advisable for us to ask for an audience. I suppose it looked as if we were going over the heads of the Sacred Congregation, or something like that.

I told Archbishop Jadot that our only intention had been to receive a blessing for the Conference. In response, we seemed to have been told that we were not an acceptable group because we were not doing or being what the Church expected of us. This appeared to me to be the obvious opinion of Cardinal Krol.

Many years later, in the fall of 2005, the memory of these events came flooding back. I learned that while Cardinal Krol was interfering in our lives with his own patriarchal ideology and spirituality of religious life, he was also at the same time moving and protecting priests in his own diocese who had been accused of pedophilia. A harsh judgment, perhaps—but also a true one.

About two months after these events, the November 5, 1973, issue of *Time* magazine printed the following bit of information, which added salt to our already smarting wound of refusal.

> The Mom of Women's Liberation, Betty Friedan, flew to Rome last week on the eve of the first meeting of the Vatican's special study commission on the role of women in society. Freidan spent four minutes in a private audience with Pope Paul VI, urging him to accord women "personhood." The Pope thanked her for the work she had done on behalf of women and accepted as a gift a brass Women's Lib symbol. Said Freidan to the Pope, "As you see, this makes a different kind of cross." Freidan avoided dogmatic issues like birth control and divorce, maintaining that "the meeting was the message." But she did have one real ideological problem: whether she should cover her head. Rejecting what she described as a symbol of women's inferiority in Judeo-Christian culture, Betty compromised on a non-hat hat—a headband.

My initial response to this incident was shock and incredulity. Was it more important for the Pope to meet with Betty Friedan and appear to affirm the values of feminism than to meet with the representatives of thousands of Catholic women religious who had given their lives to the Church? I have often wondered whether Pope Paul VI ever knew of our request for an audience. My hope was that he did not.

Our many struggles with the Sacred Congregation for Religious, and our encounters with numerous bishops, marked much of our lives in the turbulent decades immediately following the Council. We often felt dismissed, merely tolerated and even sometimes publicly corrected in one way or another.

When I was first elected to the leadership of the Conference, I went, as was the custom of Conference officials, to visit Cardinal Antoniutti, the prefect of the Sacred Congregation for Religious. Mary Daniel Turner, SSNdN, the executive director of the Conference, came with me. We were deeply offended when the Cardinal implied that now that Sister Betty Carroll RSM, a forceful and articulate leader of the Conference, had finished her term, it would be easier to deal with the organization. Betty had been a strong advocate for the contemplative nuns, and offered strong arguments and positions on many issues. When I had accompanied her the year before to our annual meeting with the prefect, she was a formidable presence, to say the least.

I found the Cardinal's remark manipulative—an attempt to play us off against each other. I suspected that he used this tactic to hide his own difficulty with having dialogue with us. His discomfort became patently obvious during the subsequent year's meeting when he instructed me to tell Sister Francis Borgia, OSF, our vice-president, that she should not be one of the editors of the new *National Catholic Reporter.* I responded that the leadership of the Conference had no authority over the internal affairs of its members' respective congregations. Furthermore, I said that we believed that Sister Francis Borgia would be an asset to the newspaper, because she was an excellent writer and editor. The Cardinal replied angrily that the *National Catholic Reporter* had "made fun of him." It turned out that the current issue featured a copy of a letter he had written to the School Sisters of Saint Francis about certain irregularities and ways of life that were deemed to be in opposition to the Council's view of religious renewal. He had insisted that a copy of the letter be sent to every house. Sister Francis responded that she could not guarantee that the letter would remain within the community if such were the case. She was ordered to disseminate it regardless. It did not remain private: the letter was printed on the front page of the *National Catholic Reporter* outlined in black, like an obituary.

The shock of meeting this kind of anger and manipulation was so grave, it shook something fundamental in me. I don't think I ever quite got over it. It did not make me bitter. It just made me feel deeply sad and disillusioned about how we as women religious were perceived. It seemed that the real issues of renewal and our dedication to the Church and its mission had become lost in concern over questions of dress and lifestyle.

I felt that way a great deal of the time during the late 1960s and early 1970s when we were going back and forth to Rome. We had many conversations and meetings with bishops, but nothing much happened to change the perception of how we were implementing in our lives the requirements of the Council. Any change in attitude seemed more the exception than the rule. Nevertheless, it must be said that a number of bishops stood with us, supported us, and encouraged us to follow our own lights, even if they did not totally understand the irrevocable path of renewal we had embarked upon.

In retrospect, I see how these encounters initiated a faith struggle within me that lasted for many, many months—even years. I had taken the documents on the Church so seriously. I had prayed about *Mystici Corporis* and *Mediator Dei* so deeply and was so nourished by the prayer of the Church, the Eucharist, the lives of its saints and martyrs. Indeed, this process had become part of the fibre of my being. Once in a while, I suspect that pursuing this love and desire for the Church is an unreal goal that denies at times the paschal mystery that is at the heart of the Church's life and being.

At a gathering of major superiors of women and men in the United States some time in the early 1970s, I gave what I thought was an ardent and forceful critique of a presentation on what the Church should be but was not, in relation to interpretations of the Council documents. I criticized what we now call the restorationist mentality. At the end of my remarks, James Walsh, a well-known Jesuit writer on discernment, asked whether he could have a word with me. Rather than offering the assurance and courage I expected, he said he hoped that I would not take it badly if he noted that my remarks appeared to come from a deep spirit of desolation rather than from a place of true hope and courage. His words provided a cold dose of truth that I would have to face many times in many ways in subsequent years.

At the same time, the commitment of women religious and of the Conference to the Church remained strong and deeply rooted during these years. We were committed to dispelling the tensions of "we" and "they" that characterized so much of the conversation. In 2004, I was able to articulate some of my thoughts from that time, when I was asked to address the Conference at its annual convention. "What would it be like if, in the Church, we owned the truth that we are 'all' the institution, even as we are 'all' the people of God?"

Perhaps, I noted in my talk, it is a stretch to appropriate the words of St. John of the Cross to acknowledge the Conference's intentionality and tenacity to name its truth, to walk in the service of leadership to further accomplish the mission of Christ in today's world. Yet in an attempt to do so, I cited the third verse of the "Spiritual Canticle" as translated by Kieran Kavanaugh, OCD. Here the soul, in search of the Beloved, will not be deterred:

> Seeking my Love,
> I will head for the mountains and for watersides,
> I will not gather flowers,
> Nor fear wild beasts;
> I will go beyond strong men and frontiers ...

Each of us involved in the renewal of religious life will need to name the "mountains and the watersides," to detect "the wild beasts" and to identify "the strong men and frontiers."

I noted that some shadowed times and events had marked our journey: for example, our own responses to the hierarchy and to the Vatican congregations. Sometimes, with the lack of clear vision that happens in cloudy times, the shadow in ourselves subtly emerges and poses as prophet, when in reality it may better reflect desolation than consolation. (For St. Ignatius, the spirit of desolation, often accompanied by lack of true vision, "rushes in rudely, violently, noisily, like rain in a storm beating on a rock, whereas consolation comes with sweetness, peace, like a drop of water on a sponge." [Spiritual Exercises, #335].)

Yet it seems to me that the same refounding spirit that animated the Conference in 1971 continues to guide and shape the directions and the understanding of who we are today and who we will be tomorrow. To borrow a phrase from the poet Gerard Manley Hopkins, the refounding spirit "shines like shook foil"—in the directions of the Conference; the topics of assemblies and their carry-over into the regions; the reflections in occasional papers; the scholarship in books and publications; in outreach to places of poverty, to missions of peace and to global concerns for sustainability and right relationships; and in brave and bold resolutions. In a special way, that same refounding spirit guides and promotes the context for relationships with the Vatican and ongoing conversations with diverse publics with which the Conference interacts to further its mission. In its 1971 statement of its purpose, the Conference articulated a new and vital perception of its meaning and mission to and in the world "to promote a developing understanding and living of religious life."

4

International Leadership Forum

Although we had our struggles with the Sacred Congregation for Religious, overall Rome was making efforts to bring together the women and men religious of the world to reflect on their mission and ministry in the post-Vatican world.

To this end, on December 8, 1965, the Sacred Congregation for Religious created the International Union of Superiors General. Its first general assembly took place in Rome on March 1 to 12, 1966. At these international gatherings, which I later attended as a councillor representing the Conference, I became more conscious of the context in which we as American religious were struggling.

Surely the fact that we were women from the United States was a factor in our more tense relationship with Rome. We had deeply internalized some of the cultural values of our country—the rights of the person, freedom and due process, and the value of democracy. We had grown up in a culture that valued dissent. I do not think that this orientation was ever fully respected, particularly by the religious culture of Rome. I often had the impression that much of what we, as Americans, said at meetings was dismissed precisely because it came from that perspective.

During the 1960s, the United States, in some ways, was cynical and negative, which affected our renewal. One of the dangers of cynicism is that it focuses on denunciation but does not call for an annunciation of hope. The critical left had a sense of what was wrong with the country, but did not tell us what was working well. That negative attitude carried over into the Church in the United States.

As religious, we became highly critical during that time—partly because of the culture we lived in, but also because we were committed to changing the social inequities of our time. Our actions did not go over well with Vatican officials. At one meeting of the International Union of Superiors General, the Pope spoke clearly in support of African and Asian religious affirming their own culture, of the importance of the Québécois affirming their French culture. Yet, nothing was said to affirm what was good in U.S. culture. The omission was not lost on us.

And yet, these gatherings taught me much about the lives and practices of women religious around the world. Those from Eastern Europe, in countries under communist occupation, were not allowed to live a public religious life or even to live in community. They faced great risks in carrying out their ministries of education or health care. Their courage made a huge impression on me. I understood what a joy it was for them to put on a habit and veil outside their countries. I also grasped their misunderstanding and disapproval of our secular dress.

In discussions with women in African congregations, I was struck by their puzzlement over conversations about the various charisms of religious groups. If they had been founded by European missionary orders, they claimed the Franciscan, Dominican or Mercy charism, as the case might be. But if a local bishop had founded their order, they struggled to name any particular distinctions or founding gift. They would say that they were called into being by a bishop who needed a group of sisters to help with the work of the diocese. They also acknowledged that, at times, one bishop could be possessive of the sisters in his diocese, not wanting them to work in another diocese.

I realized as well that, as American women religious, we were more independent than many. We had lived frugally and pooled our monies, which allowed us to build large mother houses and institutions. Unlike many women religious in Europe, we were not beholden to anyone. When Cardinal Suenens wrote *The Nun in the World*, he was addressing women religious in Europe who had lived, for the most part, in a protected environment with little or no outside contact, even though many of them were educators. Although religious life in the United States on the eve of the Council was hierarchically and monastically structured, it nevertheless integrated many of the characteristics of the cultural and democratic values of the United States. The Church in this country had been an immigrant church. Initially, it was looked upon with suspicion, but it had come to maturity through struggle and did not owe anything to anyone—particularly any government. This independent spirit would be our crowning glory as well as a significant factor in our struggle to keep naming and claiming our reality.

I recall Bishop Bernardin (not yet a cardinal) attempting to articulate, if not defend, the ethos of the U.S. Church. In the United States, he noted, when people are told either to do or not to do something, they like to know the reason why.

The International Union of Superiors General's efforts to bring together women religious from various countries are laudable, holding wonderful possibilities. Meetings in recent years are full of hope and promise. However, in the initial years, when I was a councillor, I did not find that the agenda was fully set by its officers, or that we were sufficiently consulted. It seemed to me that a kind of "Vatican aura" was too present and too controlling. I sense now that the Union's work, its questions and its agenda very much reflect major cultural, economic and political issues that both confront and challenge religious life today.

5

The Women's Movement

During my time of leadership within the Leadership Conference of Women Religious, my awareness of the situation of women—first in the Church and then more broadly, in society as a whole—became heightened. Our experience in Detroit with Cardinal Dearden in the late 1960s and early '70s had been so positive that I did not anticipate the domineering clerical leaders I would encounter as I became more active nationally and internationally. As I grew more sensitive to what appeared to me as an overbearing attitude, the patriarchal aspects of both U.S. culture and the Church became more problematic.

For a long time, I believed that the renewal of women's communities had proceeded so profoundly not because of the women's movement but because of all the work that had been done in the 1950s through the sister formation movement. When the sister formation movement began, there was no conscious connection with the emerging feminist movement. It was a turbulent time for women religious. Some of the bravest pioneers in renewal and champions for the education of women religious would later question their approach to the changing times. And so it was in my own congregation. In their later years, both the intrepid Mary Patrick Riley, IHM, and Mary Emil Penet, IHM, would struggle with grave doubts about the path that the renewal of religious life had taken. Each of them would die in a kind of dark night of the soul about the dream they had pursued so courageously—not only within the IHM congregation, but also on behalf of all women religious in the United States. Renewal had taken a turn that seemed to be at odds with their understanding of its meaning and influence in the Church and in the world.

In an article on Sister Mary Emil, Sister Joan Glisky, IHM, included some observations that Sister Mary Emil wrote in 1958, when the sister formation movement was young and full of promise. The prophetic and mystic tone of Sister Mary Emil's words offers a poignant glimpse into the heart and soul of this extraordinarily gifted woman… and what was to befall her:

> Somewhere, in all of this mighty effort which Sisters will make in the Church of our day, there is a task for me, large or small, but mine … I give myself to this task. But I know that whatever I do for God I do in the mysterious framework of our Christian destiny. If I recapitulate the life of Christ, then I will indeed accomplish little or much for a while. God will cooperate and the Palm Sundays you and I will have will be various. But the patterns of Christ's life will have to be repeated. God will seem not to cooperate all the way. Evil will seem to triumph. We will seem to be abandoned, and our work will go into eclipse. How this will come, when it will come, we do not know. But we do know that we must be ready, for the disciple is not above his Master. As a matter of fact we have never deserved to accomplish at all, and it is abundantly clear what a limitation upon our usefulness as instruments is set by our imperfections. This Christian pattern is a hard one to accept—the symbol of it is on our persons and on our walls, and we

> make the sign a hundred times a day. But we still hope that it will not have to be—or at least there is a tension in waiting. This revulsion from the cross all the time that we know we are walking toward it, all the time that, please God, we try to will to walk toward it, this is the supreme tension. Our Lord bought for us the strength to endure it with a sweat of blood.

In the 1970s, I attended a meeting at Lumen Vitae, a catechetical institute in Belgium, on changing ministries in the Church. The topic of the women's movement's influence on religious life arose. I recall saying that it was the sister formation movement, not the women's movement, that gave women religious in the United States their own voice, that spurred us on to thinking, to taking our own stand, to taking ownership for our own lives. I defended our opposition to bishops. I defended our holding our own when asked to send 20 sisters to their schools, "ready or not."

I didn't use the language of feminism then. In those early years of renewal, we did not even call ourselves "women." Universally, we referred to ourselves as "sisters." Today, however, I would say that it was indeed an emerging feminist stance that was the catalyst for renewal. Interestingly enough, a number of congregations I have noted lately speak of "our sisters" rather than "our women." An intriguing and provocative turn!

And yet, we must not underestimate the power of the sister formation movement. I had seen up close what the human, spiritual and intellectual integration of education was and had been in our congregation. I saw how it had formed young women who would become critical thinkers in the very best sense of the term. Because that kind of education was taking place at a time of cultural and spiritual upheaval, it was seen as threatening on a number of fronts.

Our problems were not caused only by men. Many women, including those with whom I served on the pastoral council of the Archdiocese of Detroit in its early years, were independent thinkers, committed to peace and justice, collaborative and articulate. However, some well-intentioned lay women who worked diligently in the Church in a number of women's groups did not agree with the changes we were embracing. These supporters of priests and bishops reflected the traditional view: to be beautifully subservient in a most gracious manner. Indeed, most bishops seemed to find such behaviour attractive. I always felt a bit of an outsider at meetings with these women. Their easy acquiescence appeared to me to be self-serving. As time went on, it became clearer and clearer that there are a variety of positions for women to take regarding their Church identity and the Church's authority as expressed in bishops and priests. All of these approaches still exist.

The 1960s and 1970s were tumultuous decades. We women religious were moving out of convents and habits and highly structured ways of life. In the midst of such a shift, it was too difficult to assess and too early to evaluate the implications of renewal.

6

Putting Down the Brush, for a While

In 1976, I finished my term as president of the congregation. When I was first elected, I was Mother Benedicta, or, more affectionately, "Mother B"; then I was Mother Margaret, then Sister Margaret. By the time I left office, I was Margaret or maybe, somewhat playfully, "Hey, you." Inwardly, I knew I was a totally different person, but I didn't know how I had gotten to where I was and had had no time to reflect on it. As I finished my term of office, I wrote the required report of my administration, describing how we had fulfilled the mandate that had been given to us from the preceding chapters of affairs. I reflected on how far we had come in renewal, and how far we still had to go. Recognizing the temptation of the time to "sit down" and stop moving ahead, I began the report with a quote from *Growth in Holiness*, by Frederick William Faber, a classical spiritual writer:

> Now is the time for courage, now is the trial of our real worth. We are beginning to travel the central regions of the renewal of our lives ... and they are, on the whole, tracts of wilderness. Here it is that so many turn back ... and here we are—together—having come to this point—toiling on, burnt by sun and wind, ankle deep

> in the sand, filled with despair from the infrequency of water springs, querulous for the want of cool, quiet shade, and greatly inclined to sit down and give the matter up as hopeless. For the love of God do not sit down. It is all over if you do.[14]

Faber's metaphor, which belonged to the spirituality of another time and place, still spoke to us about the fundamental challenge facing us. I attempted to articulate that challenge in the light of our times and from where I thought we were at that moment.

> Exactly where we are as individual persons in the achievement of our hopes and ideals—and exactly how we feel in the deepest center of our hearts, is perhaps known only to each one of us alone. The measuring of our fear—our anger and our hurt—disappointment with the Church and the congregation, with our leaders and with ourselves . . . these are the "central regions" where we may have had to confront a lack of courage or confidence, or conviction . . . a weariness and a loneliness . . . a longing at times to "let go," or "let up" or "let be."

As an introduction to my report, I wrote:

> But "where" we are, and "how" we are as a community of believers depends in no small way on the ability and the willingness to articulate that deeply personal understanding to one another. In the past decade our ecclesial perceptions have sharpened immeasurably, and the commitment of our lives to the bettering of our world has widened the dimensions of our sense of mission. We convene now as a congregation to consider these past years of our journey and to look ahead to *what* calls us to the future and to *where* that future lies. While much of the way ahead is a wilderness of long, patient perseverance—it is, above all, (and perhaps for that very reason) not a time to stop, to "settle in,"

> to sit down or simply to "tidy up." It is a call to move forward and inward—upward and outward ... in ambit of ambiguity—in the presence of paradox—submitting ourselves always to the powerful voice of God who lives in the future and who holds us in His sight.

And so it was that on June, 6, 1976, after the solemn liturgy during which the change of administration took place, I quickly and quietly left the mother house where I had lived for 24 years: fourteen in the ministry of formation and ten in leadership. I was both exhilarated and lonely, as I had been so many years before, when I left my home to come to Monroe. I slipped out of the community room where a large number of sisters were happily celebrating and congratulating the new general superior and her council. There was a lot of laughter and an ambience of great joy.

Walking down the long front corridor, I stopped for a last visit to the chapel. It was silent and dark now after the celebratory Eucharist, but the pungent odour of lilies spoke of the joyous and meaningful event that had taken place just an hour or so before. The sanctuary lamp glowed in the distance, and the single blue vigil light at the feet of Mary on the side altar cast a shadowy reflection. How many, many hours in these past 30 years had I prayed in this chapel—and with how many different emotions and concerns. It was here on July 1, 1945, that the postulant directress had led me before the altar of Mary when I entered the community. It was here before that same statue that I had, along with countless others who had gone before me, brought my doubts, my joys, my sorrows and my surrender. How many young women, and older ones, too, had confided there their fears, hopes and anguish over vocational decisions? How many professions had I presided over? How many funerals celebrating the lives of so many women, sung and unsung in the congregation's journey, had happened there?

But that night I held no sorrow, no deep concern, no urgent request—only a strange sense of leaving something behind and of embarking on a new journey—a call, I hoped, to a new place of proclamation for all that God had gifted me with these past decades.

Leaving the chapel, I continued along the corridor to the west door of the mother house, down the steps and into the car where an IHM friend was waiting to take me to another "hill country." I was hopeful that wherever I ended up, I would find an Elizabeth with whom I could sing a Magnificat, even though I was no longer a young Mary at the beginning of my life's journey.

I had ended my presidential report to the congregation with words from "Counsel for Silence," a poem by Jessica Powers, the American poet and Carmelite nun (1905–1988). As we drove away from the mother house, her words sounded in my heart with silent petition:

> Go without ceremony of departure
> and shade no subtlest word with your farewell ...

IV

Seeing and Then Seeing Again

I

The Call to Action Conference, 1976

Shortly after my term as general superior came to an end, I left the United States and spent the summer at the University of Louvain, Belgium. Two IHM sisters who were doing their doctoral studies there helped to arrange for me to participate in a special theological education program for clerics there. It was a stimulating six weeks away from Monroe; the distance was exhilarating and gave me some time to begin to internalize the theological impact of the Second Vatican Council in my own life as well as in the IHM Congregation. In the fall of 1976, I would be going to Toronto for what I thought would be a sabbatical year. One more pivotal event would take place in Detroit just a few weeks after I left for Toronto—the Call to Action Conference in the Archdiocese of Detroit, in October 1976.

In 1971, at the international synod of bishops on justice in the world, Pope Paul VI had emphasized that it was the laity, not the clergy, nor the religious, who had received the primary "call to action" that the Council had sounded in its major constitutions and decrees. The bishops attending the synod issued *Justice in the World*, a document that, I believe, is still unparalleled in its call to the whole Church:

> The Church recognizes that anyone who ventures to speak to people about justice must first be just in their eyes; hence we must undertake an examination of the modes of action, of the possession, and of the lifestyle found within the Church itself. (#40)

In response to the challenge issued by Pope Paul VI, the bishops of the United States created a consultation process of their own. They sought to call forth and to listen to the concerns of the laity. It was ten years since the close of the Council. A post-modern culture—often unreflected upon, or even consciously acknowledged—had already challenged the modern world into which the Church had entered so recently. Hearings were held in six major cities across the country so teams of bishops could listen to the hopes of the people. In Detroit, the bishops organized the Call to Action Conference.

In 1975, without waiting for the event in 1976, a group of women met in Detroit for what they thought would be a small gathering to discuss and to ask publicly, "Should women be priests?" On Thanksgiving weekend, 1,900 women met in a public forum about what would become the Women's Ordination Conference (WOC). Among the participants were a significant number of women religious. Later, the president of the National Conference of Catholic Bishops cautioned the Leadership Conference of Women Religious neither to endorse nor to attend subsequent meetings of the WOC.

In October 1976, delegates from across the country convened in the Archdiocese of Detroit under the leadership of Cardinal Dearden. In his opening address, he spoke of the powerful hearings held across the nation and of the hopes that the Call to Action Conference would engender. But above all, he called for the practice of justice, care and compassion:

> We cannot preach a justice to the world that we do not practice ourselves, we cannot demand recognition of the dignity and worth of every human person by

> governments in combating war and torture and hunger while even one person in our community is homeless, hungry or mistreated ... We must carry what we receive in and from the Church into the market place, there to redeem all of human life by participating and sharing in the struggles of humankind for dignity, justice, peace and liberation. ... For myself, I can say only one thing with full assurance, and that is that there are no clear, ready-made answers to the problems of Church and society.

As the conference progressed, I found myself pondering the Cardinal's words as converging reflections developed and took shape. Participants focused on issues that in many ways spoke of justice in areas that were central to issues of Church teaching and that touched their lives, personally and in terms of their ministry.

The 1,340 voting delegates insisted that the Catholic Church should re-evaluate its positions on issues such as celibacy for priests, male-only clergy, homosexuality, birth control, and the involvement of every level of the Church in important decisions. The delegates also declared that the Church must stand up to the chronic racism, sexism, militarism and poverty in modern society. Clearly, the participants had taken long steps ahead of the Vatican Council, although they were convinced that their stands emerged from its spirit. I think it is safe to say that a number of the bishops in attendance, although sympathetic to many of the propositions, were hesitant to discuss them within the Church. But the Call to Action Conference showed that a large number of the laity, as well as some clergy and women religious, were being challenged at a deeper level. Today, the Call to Action Conference is a formidable and influential lay-organized group. Many members of the hierarchy do not always look upon it with favour. In at least one diocese, the bishop issued an interdict on membership in the Call to Action Conference, which becomes an automatic excommunication after one month. In answer to an appeal on this tactic, the Congregation for Bishops at the Vatican issued a juridical statement that the bishop had acted within his jurisdiction.

The 1976 Call to Action Conference made me aware that my struggles with the Church would continue, but I knew I would face my struggles from a different place and space.

2

Time to Think and Think Again in Toronto

In January 1976, before I left office, I took time off to make a long retreat. I wanted to get a sense of the meaning and import of the journey I had made since that June day in 1966 when I was elected general superior. I was now 52 years old. I still had many fruitful years ahead of me. The light and darkness of those years, the successes and failures, the consolations and the desolations shifted about within me but with no discernable pattern. But one thing I knew for sure: I was a different person from the Sister Benedicta of the classical world of religious life who had become the general superior.

Around this time I happened to talk to Colin Maloney, a gifted Jesuit who was the rector of the Jesuit Theologate in Toronto. I had had a conversation with him a few years earlier, when we were searching for Jesuits to give retreats for the 1972 general chapter. I knew that he was interested in what we had done and especially why we had done it. Now, four years later, he asked me what I was going to do when I left office.

My reply was spontaneous: "Take a year to discover how I got from 'there' to 'here.'"

His response came almost immediately: "I will make you an offer that you cannot refuse."

The Jesuits were moving from their sprawling facility in the Toronto suburb of Willowdale to the downtown area to become a more integrated partner of the Toronto School of Theology, an ecumenical federation of seven theological schools that became associated with the University of Toronto. The move was also a shift from the all-inclusive in-house services of the institutional model of formation towards small residences that would foster the formation of community and include the young men in the tasks and challenges of living together, cooking, shopping and caring for the house. This new set-up would offer a major challenge to the kind of formation that had been an expected and time-honoured way of educating and forming both women and men religious as well as diocesan priests.

Regis College was a small two-storey building on the corner of St. Mary and St. Nicholas streets in mid-Toronto, within walking distance of the University of Toronto and only steps away from colourful Yonge Street with its variety of ethnic restaurants and brassy night spots. The college was truly in the heart of the city. Large apartment complexes surrounded it, housing many university students of various cultures and languages, including young families. One's Christology was easily challenged at every corner.

The Jesuits were initiating a new program at Regis that would be geared to Jesuits in their tertian year (the final stage of formation), as well as to people like me, who were leaving office in religious congregations, or diocesan priests on sabbatical. The program was designed to help participants reflect on their ministerial lives in an integrated atmosphere of theology, prayer, community, ministry and discernment.

"Would you be willing to be part of such an integrated experience and help to pilot this program," Colin asked, "and to find the space and place within which to reflect on the experience of your past ten years of leadership in the framework of such theological reflection?" Here was a new challenge for me. I was offered a scholarship to come to Toronto for a year to take part in this program. In the fall of 1976, I drove to Toronto for what I thought would be a year. I stayed for 25. I would live in Toronto longer than anywhere in my lifetime.

Living in Canada was in itself a whole new experience. Small as well as large differences struck me. I noticed, for example, that the person who got bumped in a crowd would often be the one to apologize! I saw how easily people lined up for theatres and buses, how clean the subway stations and trains were, the almost total lack of graffiti, and the absence of McDonald's, Wendy's, Burger King and 7-Eleven. No beer or liquor could be purchased on Sundays, and never in drugstores or supermarkets. Over time, almost all of these features changed. The U.S. has laid a big footprint on its neighbour to the north. Unknowingly, I began to pick up a Canadian accent. Of course, I did not know that such an accent existed. I only found this out from my family when I returned to the States for visits. My eldest brother, Richard, accosted me at one family event. "What's this with you putting on Canadian airs, with your *oots*, *aboots* and *ehs*?" he asked.

The program that I entered would, in time, become the Integration for Ministry Program. It has outlasted the many such programs of renewal, particularly several in the United States, that came into existence after Vatican II for people who had extensive experience in ministry but needed time to integrate the insights and challenges of the Council. I believe the program was so successful because it was academically rooted and because the integration process was carefully planned and executed.

The courses were constructed to touch on aspects of personal growth as well as the challenges offered by the shifts in culture that had begun so dramatically in the 1960s. Courses in world religions and liberation theology touched on the problems and promises of the world and challenged the self-absorption and supposed superiority of Western culture. Courses on the psychology of the person and the theology of conversion explored the categories described and unfolded in the work of Canadian Jesuit theologian Bernard Lonergan, which allowed students to gain insight into themselves and the world. While I never met Bernard Lonergan, I heard plenty about him. He had already moved to Boston College by the time I came to Toronto. I sensed from other Jesuits that the move from the large theologate to small-group living in the heart of the city was just not a priority for him—and that is a masterpiece of understatement, as some would say! However, a Lonergan Centre is very much a part of Regis College, where some very dedicated scholars (Jesuits and others) have been working on editing and publishing his masterful works.

Key also for the participants of this new program was a course in the spiritual exercises. These women and men could take this course to reflect on their own experience in the light of the wisdom of St. Ignatius's experience, and to search for integration in light of finding God in all things through a recommitment to the person of Jesus. A course in the New Testament grounded study in the revealed word of God. Participation in a ministry of some kind, particularly among the sick in hospitals, residents at the L'Arche House for people with developmental disabilities, or inmates in jails rooted the theology in the reality of the suffering other. Spiritual direction helped participants to clarify the meaning of these outreach opportunities. The year ended with a 30-day retreat, the culminating experience of integration.

In the first few years of the program, the participants lived in two adjacent houses owned by the Jesuits. The formation of community was a key ingredient for measuring the program's success. In those years, it was highly innovative for the women and men to live in the same house, and to share the cooking and other household tasks. Each week, the whole group met for faith-sharing, to celebrate the liturgy and to have a meal together.

The core faculty members of the program attended this weekly meeting. It was time-consuming but the effort reaped a rich reward. After several years, as the number of participants increased, the community living experience ended and community was provided for in other ways.

At the end of my year in the program, I was asked to become a member of the Regis faculty in the pastoral department, with a particular focus on the Integration for Ministry Program. This role posed a whole new set of challenges for me. For a time, I was the only non-Jesuit—not to mention the only woman—on the faculty. That in itself was a hurdle. In addition, not all the faculty had embraced the program. I think that, initially, some Jesuits hoped that the program would be an interim step that could be dispensed with once more Jesuit scholastics were ready to attend Regis. However, the program quickly became an integral part of the college curriculum. As the years passed, it grew from being a small program alongside the master of divinity program to having a stature of its own. Today, the Integration for Ministry Program has grown and expanded into several programs, diploma and full degree. Moreover, graduates of these degree programs, along with the more highly academic degree programs at Regis, receive conjoint degrees from the University of Toronto, with which Regis is affiliated.

The program also grew from one that primarily attracted religious to one that brings in predominantly lay persons. Most participants already have experience in a variety of ministries. Many have been through major transitions in their lives. They seek to name this transition and integrate it through the reflections that the program's key courses and integrative seminar invite.

The Jesuits I met at Regis College struck me immediately as a "freer breed" than those I had known in Detroit or in the States in general. Not one wore a clerical collar or dressed in black. Rather, they dressed in suits or sport jackets, with shirts and ties of various styles and colours. I learned, in time, that only on "state occasions"—formal clerical gatherings in the diocese—did they don "clericals." Even then I am not sure they all conformed. When I arrived in Canada, the 25th general congregation of the Society of Jesus was in session. It was a stormy time. In the United States, a number of discussions on the subject were being held in Jesuit institutions. I asked Jean-Marc Laporte, SJ, the president of Regis, if the Canadian Jesuits were involved in the same way. His laid-back, sensible response seemed characteristic of Canadians as a whole—at least in my experience. "Canada is a winter country," he said, somewhat facetiously. "When there is a storm, we just batten down the hatches and wait for it to pass."

Some of my colleagues were not enthusiastic about having a female presence in what had for so long been an exclusively male clerical enterprise. As I took up my new responsibilities, for example, I did not have my own office. I will always remember the kindness and graciousness of David Stanley, SJ, the renowned scripture scholar, semi-retired at the time, who offered to share his office with me. Later, when he retired and it became fully my own, I refused to take his name off the door out of my deep respect for him. However, by the time I left Regis so many years later, I knew that I was accepted and respected as an integral member of the faculty, which by then had expanded to include more women and laity.

A key experience for me in the development of the Integration for Ministry Program was working in those early years with Ron Barnes SJ, who died in 2003, and Peter Fitzpatrick, CFX, a Xaverian brother who later returned to the United States to take up leadership in his own community. I found working and planning with men refreshing and challenging; our relationship continued long after we had ceased to be part of the program. In time, the administration of the program added new dimensions. It grew and flourished under the wise and dedicated directorship of Cathleen Flynn, CSJ.

Living in Toronto was like experiencing a slice of the whole world. I knew that after the Second World War, an influx of immigrants had poured into Canada, but I was unprepared for the ethnic and religious differences that met me on every street corner. While I had lived all of my life just south of the Canadian border, I had no real sense of Canada's cultural and political reality. Canada, for many Americans, was a summer playground—a wonderful vacation place of beautiful lakes and campgrounds as well as cultural opportunities such as the Shakespearean festival each year in Stratford. It startled and embarrassed me that U.S. students coming into the program (myself included!) could name neither the Canadian provinces nor the elected officials, nor did they know how the country functioned.

Regis College's ecumenical landscape (as part of a federation of seven theological schools) was another eye-opener for me. Growing up, being educated, and living and ministering in an exclusively Catholic environment, I had next to no involvement in any other religious context. Moreover, and perhaps more surprisingly still, I had never taught a non-Catholic, and had never even had a serious conversation with a Protestant. Having colleagues who came from other Christian traditions and other faiths as well was exhilarating. Not that all this newness was easy: it was extremely challenging.

Teaching at Regis and in the Toronto School of Theology became a time of real stretching in my life. The early creative years in the development of the program were rich and rewarding. Later, I was offered positions both at Boston College and in the Jesuit School of Theology at Berkeley, California. My IHM community and my family could not understand why I would stay in Canada when I could be in such vibrant U.S. cities. Nevertheless, I knew that I had very good reasons.

It was healthy for me to be away from the IHM congregation and from the politics of the United States, and to open myself up to new horizons. Working with adult students from a variety of cultures shaped my perceptions of the world and made me aware of my unconscious bias that saw the United States and its expression of Western culture as the norm and model. I remember well one day in class when I spoke of the Far East. An Indonesian student politely and insightfully asked, "East of *where*, Professor Brennan?"

I became particularly close to the Korean students, most of whom were Presbyterian. They were very eager and industrious, and possessed a kind of spiritual curiosity that challenged me. I felt that they often taught me much more than I taught them.

At Regis, I also found it a source of never-ending growth to teach lay women and lay men, with whom I had had so little contact. To hear how they discovered God in their lives—in marriage, through childbirth, in relationships in the workplace, as well as in daily family life and childrearing—was a constant source of wonder to me, who had spent so much of my life involved in the struggles and joys of the institutional Church and of religious life.

In addition, I had the opportunity to team teach with some of my Jesuit colleagues, and eventually with non-Jesuits who joined the faculty. I was so stimulated by my teaching and so enjoyed it that at first it seemed wrong to accept a salary for my work (I got over this feeling when it came time to pay the bills and help meet the financial needs of my own community). For the first time, at age 52, I began to form deep and lasting friendships outside of my IHM life. These relationships called forth sides of me that had been untouched all my adult life. My horizons expanded in directions that I would not have thought possible after the challenging and mind-expanding time in leadership in the post-Vatican years.

My time in Toronto revealed the workings of the Church in Canada, which was not the same as the Church of the U.S. I learned, for example, especially through the writings of theologians such as Gregory Baum, that the social gospel had a much stronger impact in Canada than in the U.S. and that the Christian churches worked much more closely on the moral implications of the political, economic and social life of the country. A lasting impression I carry about Gregory was that I never, ever heard him speak negatively about the Church or about his painful experience with Rome that resulted in his leaving the priesthood. He sometimes said that Catholics would be less angry with the

Church when they stopped looking for the "perfect mother." He was also fond of saying that if you were never criticized for what you delivered in a lecture or talk, then very likely you had not had much to say! One summer, we were both teaching at the Pastoral Institute at Boston College during the same three-week period. He and his wife, Shirley, lived in one of the senior apartments next door to where I was staying. They were both solicitous and caring, and more than once I joined them for dinner or an evening in Boston. One morning as I was walking to my class, laden with books and mimeographed outlines for the students, I caught up with Gregory. He was sauntering along in his Bermuda shorts and sandals, on his way to a three-hour class without so much as a book in his hand. To my incredulous question of how he could possibly handle such a daunting task without a single paper to refer to, he wisely said, "Well ... you know (with a little lilt in the "know" and a slight German accent) ... in a summer course one can only comment on one stone of a large mosaic, not the whole work of art." This was a wonderful piece of wisdom that I took to heart.

For some years while at Regis, I was on the editorial board of *Catholic New Times*, an independent biweekly grassroots newspaper not unlike the *National Catholic Reporter*. This experience taught me about how Canadians dealt with conflict, pursued issues of social and moral import, and viewed the United States.

During my time in Toronto, I also learned about the difference in the way that American and Canadian women religious handled the challenges they faced. I was all too familiar with the struggle of American women religious to work as teachers in the parochial school system, earning low salaries, no pensions, and no social security until the 1970s. Meanwhile, some Canadian provinces had long-standing agreements that the government would fund Catholic education. In Canada, I found that women religious did not have to fight for just conditions for their schools. I now understood how it was that U.S. women religious often appeared to be pushy or feisty compared to our Canadian sisters and colleagues.

Perhaps one of the greatest learning experiences I had in my Canadian years was teaching a course to Aboriginal students at Anishinabi, a Jesuit centre in Ontario for Aboriginal people. I was solicited to teach this course by Carl Stenkloff, SJ, an American Jesuit who was now at Regis but had spent many fruitful years working with Aboriginal people in Wyoming. Coincidentally, IHM sisters taught in the reservation's school. The Regis project, sponsored by the Jesuits, aimed to enhance collaboration with Aboriginal people and promote the kind of theology that reverences the growing self-awareness of the Aboriginal Church. Preparing Aboriginal deacons for ordination was part of this endeavour; a major challenge around the issue of Aboriginal clergy and leadership was to address concerns about the quality of seminary education and the question of clerical celibacy.

The course I was to teach was Theology of Ministry. I had eight students. Never having taught Aboriginal people before, I was unprepared for what I perceived to be a lack of enthusiasm and the kind of immediate responses that I was used to. The students seemed to be studying me and listening to me from a deep place that I could not enter. This was the 1980s—ecological questions and a sense of cosmic consciousness were not yet a part of theological discussions in any serious way. The early writings of such authors as Matthew Fox and Thomas Berry were, for the most part, not considered sound theology. When I mentioned to the students that it was only human beings among all God's creatures who could respond consciously to God and to one another, one of the students asked a question. His statement of deep conviction came more from experience than expertise. "I don't know about that, Sister. Don't you think that the wind speaks to the trees?" Here was the beginning of a whole new trend of thought for me. It has become part of my thinking on cosmic consciousness and its implications for the future of our planet, and the corresponding challenge to the Church.

3

Coming to Terms with Feminist Spirituality

Teaching at Regis offered me an opportunity to reflect critically on the experiences I had had as a woman in the Church. I had time to read and absorb the recent writings of feminist theologians—about how human experience, in addition to scripture and tradition, was a source of revelation. Such a realization happened over a long period, as seeds of new experience began to grow. In the summer of 1985, I set out my thoughts in an article in the journal *The Way* entitled "Women and Theology: Singing of God in an Alien Land." Much of the following reflection comes from that article.

Although I had studied theology as a young woman, it was my decade of ministry in IHM administration and leadership that proved to be my real theological education. It enabled me to bring to my teaching at Regis College some grounded insights on the emerging role of women in service to the Church. I knew first-hand, intimately, what it meant to internalize the renewed theology of the Church and its role in the modern world.

The frustrating and often disheartening attempts to share that experience with Vatican authorities had led to sharp disagreements that would only deepen as the years passed. The women's movement of the 1960s had found its way into the Church, with a growing insistence and desire on the part of women for fuller participation in the Church's life and mission. The Church's teaching, I believed, would now have to be integrated regarding the place and position of women in the Church. In many ways, this belief would influence my teaching and my understanding of the students who took my classes. My reflection on and study of spirituality in the past had inclined me to believe that spirituality had generally been presented within a framework of values traditionally associated with men—individuation, separateness and the quest for glorious achievement.

I took time to set out my thoughts in the midst of my teaching. Images of ladders and scales of perfection, levels of detachment and stages of prayer to be achieved by set rules and formulas or feats of asceticism were the blueprint for arriving at a state of undivided love of God. Human love was in some way in competition with love for God: building the kingdom of God through establishing or contributing to institutions for education, health care and evangelization were the hallmarks of our zeal.

My experience as a woman theologian was enriched by getting to know my students and by the easy access I had to the developing literature of feminist scholars. At the same time, my personal theological questions came to the fore. My efforts and energies were focused on creating courses, dealing with student concerns, developing and promoting the program, and receiving intellectual stimulation. For all its seductiveness, such stimulation could be suffocating. Time for personal reflection and the probing of my own experience was frequently set aside, or, more dangerously, caught up in immediate self-consciousness, which is easily confused with contemplation. The receiving sides of me were closed off. The core of my life was unheard and unattended to.

Then, unexpectedly, a vivid childhood memory surfaced. It named an emotion that I had been either unable or unwilling to articulate: fear, accompanied by a sense of impending loss that left me feeling outside of myself.

One day, when I was four or five years old, I climbed onto the side of the bathtub and then on to the edge of the pedestal sink in order to see myself in the bathroom mirror. It was a warm spring day. The window was open: I felt the fresh breeze that gently blew through the curtains and saw the sun on the uppermost branches of the trees in the backyard. However, the general warmth and sensuality of the experience gave way to a feeling that seemed to clutch at my heart. I gazed intently in the mirror and wondered, "What if there is no God?" I do not know where the question came from. I can recall no event or experience that might give it meaning. Yet I distinctly remember the fear and uneasiness that surrounded it.

What brought back that childhood memory and the feeling it engendered was an experience that uncovered the same clutching fear and sense of loss. The difference was that now I could name it and knew its source.

When I began to read the work of Christian feminist thinkers, I did so with intellectual curiosity coupled with a growing conviction that was forming my mind but had not yet touched deep religious levels in terms of my relationship with God. While I was claiming the insights of feminist theology and bringing them into my teaching, my own relationship to God had not fundamentally changed nor been challenged. I still moved, lived and prayed in the warmth and comfort of the one anchor in a theological world that had shifted dramatically, though I did not realize it. An internal change had taken place in me, but I had not attended to it. Then one day, like the four- or five-year-old of decades past, I looked at myself intently, in the mirror of my spirit. A question arose that gripped my heart with the fear and sense of loss I had known once before. The God I had related to with such assurance and confidence no longer lifted my heart in joy and loving surrender. Instead, I felt incredible sadness and fear, an empty space in which my unuttered question searched for a voice with a frightened, inarticulate cry: "Who and where is God for me now?" The symbols and names of God that had guided my prayer now had alien sounds. The image I had of myself was merely a reflection. I set about exploring the question.

It is my belief that every woman who has seriously grappled with feminist theology and considered her own value and story has had a similar experience. The circumstances may vary, but not the essence. The awareness that one has related to a God who has been consistently named and symbolized in masculine terms, in a Church that has subordinated women and devalued their gifts, has provoked a crisis in many hearts and minds. The resolution of this crisis has spawned a growing volume of literature that attests to a renaming of God arising from a new, richer experience.

Highly educated women equipped with the required skills have challenged the theological structures of a classical disembodied spirituality that had found its way into the articulation of dogma and magisterial teaching. Women have offered new perspectives and insights that can, I hope, lead to creative and alternative ways of doing theology.

For me, Christian feminism was not intended to produce a separatist movement or to create a female God to replace and unseat the male deity of patriarchy and my upbringing. Rather, the aim of Christian feminism is to recover, reclaim and rename the God who is not any one person or any one thing, but is the source and the reality of all persons and all things.

With the question "Who and where is God for me now?" in mind, I began a sabbatical year in Boston in 1984. A great and yawning space had closed about and above me. One evening, I reflected on "Gestalt at Sixty," a poem by a contemporary woman writer, May Sarton. Its message struck a familiar chord, unleashing sounds in me that had been silent and inarticulate all these years. In the poem, Sarton says that "solitude / Is not all exaltation, inner space / Where the soul breathes and work can be done." Rather, "The past, never at rest, flows through it."

Left to myself in Boston, I discovered that the question I had dealt with so convincingly in classes and with colleagues rose up from nameless currents in my own spirit. I had to climb down from the heady arguments of my mind to meet them in the turmoil of my heart. I was filled with insistence about the need to rename and reclaim the feminine in God, and resistance to the masculine symbols and titles that made God a patriarch, a king, a warrior or champion. Yet my heart had found no homeland for these convictions. I was wandering in a desert land.

During this sabbatical year, I planned to engage in some Jungian analysis as well as spiritual direction. For many years, I had used the insights of Carl Jung in aspects of my teaching, but had had no personal experience of dream analysis or getting in touch with archetypal symbols and their power to reveal hidden sides of the psyche. It seemed to me that a combination of such inner journeying, along with more reading in what I call frontier areas of theology, would be a rich and rewarding use of my time.

Daveda, my Jungian analyst, was a Jewish woman. I do not think that she was religious in any credal sense, but as I came to discover, she was one of the most religious people I had ever met—reverent, respectful and deeply in touch with the inner life of all things collectively, and of each thing individually.

Kieran, my spiritual director, was a Mercy sister who worked at a retreat house in Rhode Island. I had known her for some years, but from a distance. When I met her again during my sabbatical, she was in remission from bone cancer. She had been very close to death, not once, but twice. It was this experience, I believe, that gave her the sense of the freedom of spirit and detachment with which she viewed the deep and heavy questions of life and of the Church. She had seen things from the other side, as it were, and could put them in perspective.

Daveda challenged me to expand the horizons of my world of meaning. From her, I learned how deeply I was "caught up in the collective" (her word for Church), how attached I was to my own images of how and what the Church should be, and how angry I was with Roman authorities and bishops.

As often happens in analysis, relating what seemed to be a simple incident brought meaning and insight. One afternoon, when visiting with Daveda, I recalled, somewhat casually, a conversation I had had during the week with my Carmelite friend Connie Fitzgerald. I had read that the Carmelites had had a serious setback in pursuing their renewal. This was many years after the promise of the groundbreaking 1969 meeting in Woodstock, Maryland, of contemplative nuns in the United States and Canada. I saw this recent setback as unjust and incomprehensible. Connie's quiet response to my insistent and repetitive question, "But what are you going to *do* about it?" came as a bit of a shock. The Carmelites, she said, would make no public response. Difficult as it might be, they would quietly keep discerning and pursuing their renewal while recognizing that their commitment to their charism might be perceived as disobedience. Daveda told me I shouldn't be so surprised. "After all," she said, "Connie is older than you are."

"Oh, but she is not," I said. "I am at least ten years older than she is."

"That is not what I meant," she said.

Suspiciously, I asked, "Well, what *did* you mean?"

"You," she rejoined, "are like an adolescent raging and confronting the authority of a father whom you do not want to obey. Connie, on the other hand, responds like an adult. She listens carefully and respectfully, but then reflects on what she knows is best for her."

Not a very flattering image to be faced with at age 60! Yet Daveda's response was the kind of adult reaction that appeared to be missing from my own approach.

On the side of faith, Kieran challenged me to put aside for a time—if I could—the God I had come to know through my religious formation, the formulations of theology and even the revelation of scripture. She encouraged me to open myself to the infinite flow of God and to God, who is the infinite capacity in myself to receive infinity. This God is not poverty, celibacy, obedience, not social justice, not the institutional Church, not feminist theology.

Meister Eckhart's prayer "I pray thee God to rid me of God" became a kind of unspoken attitude of supplication as I sought to let go of the images that were anchored in my mind but that no longer spoke to my heart. But letting go, I learned, was not something that I could simply make up my mind to do. Letting go is something that happens organically as old images are healed and transformed, and fresh ones slowly take shape out of new awareness, perception and experience. This evolution began, I believe, through two related movements that have been growing in both power and influence during the last two decades: the healing and transformation of patriarchal images of God through a deeper understanding of sexuality and spirituality, and the understanding of God's creation and our place in it—not only through biblical accounts and tradition but especially through modern physics and ecology.

I do not believe that the male images of God that are so deeply rooted in our Christian psyche, perhaps irrevocably, need to disappear altogether. However, unless those symbols are freed from the dominant power of patriarchy through healing and transformation that restores their true meaning (and makes room for other images as well), they become increasingly alienating to women and men alike.

In spite of protestations to the contrary, androcentric values in the Catholic Church have resulted in an exclusive masculine naming of God in official Church teaching, in the choice of the liturgical texts that surround its worship, and in the exclusive modelling of ministers who mediate its sacramental life. The male symbol has become the reality. It has given men a role model not afforded to women.

Furthermore, this male imaging, as it is reflected in the statements of authority figures in the Church, is one of domination, a posture increasingly repugnant to men as well as women. To dissent is not only to be disloyal, but also, according to the Congregation for the Doctrine of the Faith's recent document *On the Ecclesial Vocation of the Theologian*, subversive: "To succumb to the temptation of dissent ... is to allow the leaven of infidelity to the Holy Spirit to work" (no. 40).

The projected authority of God that stands behind such pronouncements reflects a kind of command hierarchy in the great chain of being. God tells the Church officials what to do, they tell us, and we obey. To quote theologian Dorothee Soelle, we are asked "to honor a God whose most important attribute is power, whose prime need is to subjugate, whose greatest fear is equality."[15] Such a view suggests a failure to imagine mutuality and egalitarian partnership, a collaborative model of Church. This view is also an outright denial of the Second Vatican Council's endorsement of the diversity of gifts within the Church's life and the exercise of its mission. In the process, such a viewpoint legitimates oppression.

When Christian feminists began to reverence their own bodies as sources of grace and goodness—to view them as symbols of God's nurturing and life-giving essence and power rather than sources of temptation, seduction and distraction—they set the stage for a new spirituality and a new experience of God. Fresh understandings of themselves and of their relationships to others, to the world, and to the transcendent were enhanced when they shared their stories. They heard each other into speech. They found the voice they needed to claim spiritual equality, recovering the symbol of the feminine that had been both degraded and relegated to the realm of the ethereal eternal feminine that had nothing to do with real life.

The recovery of the symbol of the feminine—of "embodiness"—coincides easily with the insights of postmodern physicists who speak of the cosmos as a living entity in which all forms of life are connected in probability patterns of energy that flow through everything equally. The images of the mystics, who sense our profound embodiness, can aid us in our own search and struggle to name such new awareness. This certainly was the case for me.

During my sabbatical, I was able to name in a more profound way what the previous eight years at Regis had brought about in me, in terms of relating spirituality and sexuality. For the first time since my early life at home, I found myself living in a male world. Doing spiritual direction with seminarians, priests and lay men (single and married) took me beyond books and theories about the differences between men's and women's spirituality.

In the fall of 1985, I returned to Regis. By now, I had found a side of myself that had developed independently from my IHM roots and had some critical distance from the situation of women religious in the United States.

In 1993, I was unexpectedly called back into the reality of the Leadership Conference. The National Conference of Catholic Bishops, at its national meeting in Dallas on June 18, 1993, had issued an invitation to both the male and female conferences of religious to deliver a response to the *Lineamenta,* a document prepared in Rome on the role of religious, which was to be discussed at the upcoming Synod on Religious Life. I was asked by the Leadership Conference to make such a response in its name. This response would have more dire consequences than I ever dreamed. For the most part, I responded favourably to the challenges proposed in the document and how those challenges could contribute to the ongoing relationship between women religious and bishops. I passed my response by several major superiors of women for their critique and suggestions before delivering it.

However, I did make one criticism that I feared might not be well received by all the bishops. Nevertheless, I took my chances, and discovered only sometime later that my fears were well grounded.

> While the *Lineamenta*, in citing *Mutuae Relationes*, acknowledges the distinctive gifts that women religious bring to the Church in response to the concrete need of both the Church and the world (#19), it also notes that "in some cases a mistaken idea of feminism has laid claim to the right to participate in the life of the Church in ways which are not in keeping with the hierarchical structure willed by Christ." (L #29)

To this statement, I responded that "It must be said that a statement of such dogmatic certitude will appear to many women as one that denies our birthright as baptized Christians to be church as women, and denies women any role in decision-making bodies." I further noted the following:

> It is important for you as bishops to understand that the commitment of many women religious to the feminist movement in the Church is not to overthrow our rich tradition but rather to challenge and to overcome the dualisms that have taken root in the structures and its symbol system as well. An emerging feminist consciousness has enabled us to invite others into an expanded experience of God and our world. This is particularly true in the way that women theologians have been able to revision our Christian tradition and to bring feminist theology to a new level of consciousness. In this area we cherish the hope that continued theological reflection and dialogue can open wider vistas of inclusion that lead to a discipleship of equals. Though efforts to produce a United States Bishops pastoral on women's concerns were not successful, such efforts cannot have been totally in vain. Hopefully, you as bishops can and

> will continue the struggle to make operative its closing statement that "the equality of women and men is not a privilege to be earned by anyone but a reality belonging to all by virtue of our creation in the image of God and our redemption by Christ Jesus" (*One in Christ Jesus*, National Conference of Catholic Bishops, #56).

The bishops did not allow or provide for the discussion of responses to the *Lineamenta*; they merely received them. It was sometime later that I learned that because my remark was considered to be critical of the hierarchy, my name was included on the list of "undesirable" speakers in my own archdiocese of Detroit for some time.

4

Seeing Through Prayer

The years passed. I had learned a great deal about Canada, the world, and the Jesuit Order. I had taught at Regis under three presidents and the provincial. Most of all, I had formed deep and lasting friendships outside of my IHM life and community.

By the fall of 2001, I was 77 years old and professor emerita at Regis. I had been in Toronto for 25 years. I was still teaching one or two courses per semester, but an insistent small voice began to sound with increasing clarity, telling me it was time to leave. I wanted to go when I thought (and hoped!) that the faculty and students still wanted me to stay. I did not want to be a relic of the past or to fear or imagine my colleagues saying to one another, "*When* is she leaving?" Nevertheless, it was a difficult decision.

My last year was meaningful: I left with an honorary degree and was privileged to give the graduation address. My close friends at the college held a wonderful closing dinner, which a number of my family attended.

The students celebrated my years at Regis in a special assembly. I was particularly touched when a group of Korean students sang a song from their homeland expressing love and gratitude. They presented me with two carved traditional Korean *tal* (masks), male and female. The *tal* is the face of *minjung*, which expresses *han*. *Han* is the wounded hearts of the poor people. The *tal* has a smiling face, but if you look at the mask for a long time, you will feel the sorrow. Behind the smiling face lies the collective suffering of the oppressed. Therefore, the *tal* is a way for the people to transcend their reality by performing the mask dance. These two beautifully carved wooden masks hang on the wall in my place of study, an ever-present reminder of the Canadian sojourn that so influenced my life.

I sorted out my library and left many books behind under a "free to take" sign. Very early on a December morning, a moving van came first to my apartment and then to the college to pick up my boxes. A good friend and colleague, Kathleen McAlpin, RSM, accompanied me on the five-hour drive to Farmington Hills, Michigan. The trip was uneventful, until we arrived at customs in Sarnia, Ontario. I did not expect the emotional reaction I felt when the officer required me to "relinquish my papers," which meant that I could no longer go and come into the country that had been my home for so long.

Several weeks after my return to Michigan, I travelled to Majorca, off the coast of Spain, to make a 30-day retreat with a Jesuit friend. Valentin Romallo, SJ, was a wise and gifted interpreter of the Ignatian spiritual exercises whom I had met many years before in Toronto. As I journeyed through the exercises once again, I looked long and hard at what retirement might mean for me, and what it would ask of me. Two scripture passages became the heart of my reflections, touching sensitive areas that will challenge me for the rest of my days.

They both had to do with challenges of the heart—of the *being* of my life, not the *doing*.

The first is the story of Martha and Mary in Luke 11:1-4. A trap and temptation for me, as the reader of this book may now know, is to complain about the Church and to mourn over it—how it should or should not be, what it is doing or not doing. Jesus' words to the zealous but troubled Martha resonated deep within me. "Martha, Martha, you are worried and troubled over many things ... but only one thing is necessary ...." As my Spanish director would say so often, "Una cosa es necessario."

The second passage is from John 21:18, which records the words of the Risen Jesus to Peter on the shore of the lake:

> I tell you most solemnly, when you were young you put on your own belt and walked where you liked; but when you grow old you will stretch out your hands, and someone else will put a belt round you and take you where you would rather not go.

Will I indeed be able to go where I would rather not? I wondered. And will I even have a choice?

The full meaning of these passages continues to challenge me. To be able to let go of how and what and where the Church, my religious congregation, and I should be is an almost daily preoccupation that I can easily mistake for zeal. When it arises, I often return to the words of Daveda, my Jungian analyst in 1984, and try not to be so "caught up in the collective."

Ron Barnes was a Jesuit friend and colleague of mine in Toronto. I had taught with and pestered him with my preoccupations about the Church for many years. Standing at his bedside in the Jesuit infirmary as he lay dying, I found myself mentioning my hopes or my latest struggle or disappointment with the Church. A bit wearily he smiled, caught my eye, shook his head and said, "You never give up, do you?" His comment was not intended as a compliment. Now, he knows and experiences the reality of it all, and I expect that he is either on my side or helping me to move to another!

V

What Is There for Me Now

1

Making Adjustments

I took up residence in an IHM house in Farmington Hills, a suburb of northwest Detroit. I had stayed there many times before. A dear and long-time friend, Lorraine Humphrey, IHM, with whom I had travelled in Vietnam years earlier, made me feel instantly at home. It is a wonderfully welcoming place for IHM sisters who come to Detroit to attend meetings at the IHM mother house in Monroe or at our college in Detroit. These sisters hail from such places as Texas, Kentucky, Minnesota, Indiana and other areas. The house is a gathering place where a great cross-section of stimulating conversation takes place.

During my years at Regis, I had visited Detroit dozens of times. But moving back there with my boxes and my books was a big adjustment. I was back, but not yet "at home." Toronto is a multicultural mecca, the world within a city, home to nearly five million people from more than 80 ethnic groups. In one of the highrises next to Regis College, graduate students from the University of Toronto, many with young families, spoke more than 90 languages. A walk to the College from where I lived could easily generate ten new ideas. People from different areas of the world could be found on every corner.

When Honey (Sister Lorraine's nickname) said to me encouragingly, "Marg, you are going to love it here. Everything you need is on the corner," my heart sank. "On the corner," indeed! The small strip mall, a few streets away, boasts a Rite Aid drugstore, a Hallmark store, a Greek family restaurant (very good!), a beauty parlour, Heartland Grocery, a florist, UPS, a Blockbuster Video, a gas station and, to really make me feel at home, a Tim Horton's coffee and doughnut shop! The post office and community library, as well as a YMCA, are within walking distance. It took time, but gradually I put down some tender roots.

The suburban area in which I lived made its own statement about community and neighbourliness. The IHM house on Kendallwood Drive is on a winding street that has no sidewalks. None of the houses have front porches. Patios and recreational swings and slides are located behind and away from the street. Although there are at least three elementary schools and therefore many children in the area, I rarely see children playing in the street or in front of their houses. I suspect that most of them join in organized play at school, the Y, or other soccer, basketball or swimming clubs.

Adjusting to suburbia was one thing. More significant was the general cultural reality of "empire." Canadians are highly aware of this reality; I often found myself defending the U.S. position when I lived in Canada. To my surprise, I found that I was now looking at my own country through Canadian eyes and my Canadian of 25 years. I became more aware of critiques of multinationals and their control of foreign markets and the economies of poorer countries. I was enmeshed in the shame of U.S. actions at Abu Ghraib prison in Iraq, and recoiled at our defence of the use of some forms of torture. I became more sensitive to the plight of immigrants and was horrified when U.S. presidential candidate John McCain stated that the United States could be in Iraq for a hundred years. Reading sound and challenging critiques of America by American writers and thinkers helped me see that my view of the U.S. had changed.

Indeed, learning to feel at home once again in this city of my roots, upbringing and education proved to be a greater challenge than I had anticipated. The demographics had changed considerably, even since 1976, when I left for Toronto. Life in the suburbs is a far cry from life in downtown Detroit. The first "white flight"—an exodus of white residents—occurred in the 1950s, when the government had offered easy loans to returning Second World War veterans and their families. More whites left the downtown area as a result of the racial upheavals of the 1960s. Moreover, a number of freeways and expressways now crisscrossed the city, causing the depreciation of many neighbourhoods and leaving them, for the most part, to poorer blacks and Hispanics. An inadequate public transportation system made it difficult or impossible to travel from one neighbourhood to another. The racial upheavals also left entire areas of the city burned out or abandoned. Meanwhile, large subdivisions populated mostly by whites appeared almost overnight in areas that once were countryside. Valiant attempts to rebuild the downtown have taken place, but the suburbs continue to stretch out to both the northeast and northwest of the city into new townships. New churches (both Catholic and evangelical), along with new educational facilities, naturally follow in the wake of this migration. The quality of public education has diminished, as fewer teachers venture into the city schools. Abandoned school buildings are a familiar sight. The once numerous parochial Catholic schools are almost non-existent. In 2006, the Archdiocese closed fifteen Catholic high schools. Many Catholic churches have closed as well.

And yet, I remain heartened by my own congregation's explicit statements of support and ministry within the city of Detroit, and by our ongoing commitment to our own Marygrove College, which once was part of a healthy middle-class neighbourhood, but is now deep in the heart of the outer boundaries of a struggling city.

My sister Ellen often recalls that our father used to say that "the automotive industry had made the city of Detroit, and would one day destroy it." His prophetic words are close to becoming reality. "Motown," the nickname for this "motor city," is feeling the effects of the growing financial crises of the three great automakers: Ford, General Motors and Chrysler. Massive layoffs and downsizing, as well as the closing of production plants and corporate offices, have left a somber mood in the city. A number of IHM sisters continue to minister or simply live in solidarity with those who call Detroit home during this bleak time.

The IHM house in Farmington Hills is almost midway between two other suburbs, where my two remaining sisters live. I have been able to connect with them in ways that we had not been able to do in many years. Within walking distance is a vibrant parish, St. Fabian's, where I have taken up the roles of lector, commentator, altar minister, and occasional speaker. Here, those of us who have taken on these ministries have been made to feel that what we do is an important part of the daily and Sunday celebrations of liturgy. As a lector, I am once again highly aware of the lack of inclusive language in the official books we use in the liturgy each day. My personal commitment to make changes has either not been noticed or has been noticed but not commented on!

Here in the parish, I have met a wonderful group of lay women and men who are led and encouraged by an enterprising and dedicated pastor. He enables this hard-working parish team to create a community of service and worship. The pastoral assistant, a most capable and energetic lay woman, co-ordinates events and liturgical schedules. With great ease, she, along with the business administrator, moved the parish forward with no major incidents while the pastor was away in Rome for a well-deserved sabbatical and time for some theological updating. Each week, parish volunteers serve in soup kitchens and other places of ministry. Each year, the parish takes part in an archdiocesan project of offering shelter and food to homeless people, as part of a city-wide program, Housing the Homeless. Once a year, the large school gym is transformed into sleeping areas for people who are homeless. Many generous and dedicated parishioners tend to the people's needs. Also, a youth group travels to Appalachia to help in the work of Habitat for Humanity. Members of the Christian Service Committee, along with a neighbouring parish, volunteer service to Rebuilding Together, a national program through which local citizens repair local homes. Here, people ages 12 and up work together.

These are just a few of the events and opportunities of this dynamic parish, which is not unlike a number of others in the suburbs and elsewhere in the city, where other parishes serve the poor in shelters and soup kitchens.

The diocese unites groups of neighbouring parishes and informs parishioners of a number of Catholic social services in such areas as family support services, foster care and adoption. Yet, even here, I sense that the archdiocese is not fully aware of the diminishment that confronts us as parishes are closed and others are merged. Perhaps it is not so much a lack of awareness but rather a case of doing one's best and pretending not to notice. Parishes are merging not only because of a lack of parishioners, who keep moving away into newly created suburbs and leaving older parishes with diminishing numbers. More problematic is the lack of clergy. Most priests minister in a parish alone, without a community of fellow priests to offer support.

And yet, Church leaders seem to have no desire to discuss the key question of personnel, aside from making a play for lay men to enter the diaconate program. Periodically, in one way or another, we are reminded that celibacy is not optional for the priesthood, and that the question of the ordination of women, even to the diaconate, is closed. Homosexuality, according to Church authorities, is "disordered." Even to be a public speaker or occasional lecturer, one must pass the litmus test of orthodoxy. This means that membership in the Call to Action Conference is not encouraged (ironic, given that the first Call to Action Conference took place in this archdiocese in the time of Cardinal Dearden), nor are conferences or speakers that might promote the ordination of women.

Most of the men who enter the seminary here (as in many others across the country) tend to reflect the revisionist mentality of John Paul II, with its criticism of how Vatican II has been interpreted. As a result, in my perception, strong and innovative leadership among the laity does not seem to be a priority, and generally is not encouraged. And, where leadership of the laity does not exist, some lay women and men gather for mutual encouragement. The exception is parishes in which pastors have been able to successfully steer a tricky passage, or among grassroots groups whose theology reflects the early hopes and promises of Vatican II. As a result, a significant number of laity feel alienated from Church structures and institutions that do not deal in a forthright manner and in depth with serious issues and concerns.

A few years ago, in May 2006, I felt the strong hand of authority in my own life, just when I thought that such times were long past for me. Sister Mary McDevitt, IHM, was now on the teaching faculty of Sts. Cyril and Methodius Seminary, located in the outlying suburb of Orchard Lake near Detroit. She was offering a course on Catholic spiritual traditions, and asked me to teach a class on the Carmelite mystical tradition, which I had taught often. Although the class was primarily for seminarians, Mary posted it as a public lecture. Two days before the lecture, the rector told her to cancel the class. He had received (anonymously) information from the Internet stating that in 1978, I had participated on a panel about Church order—that is, the ordering of ministries—at the second Women's Ordination Conference in Baltimore. Yet Pope John Paul II's strong admonition not to discuss the ordination of women was issued ten years after the conference at which I spoke! What is more, my point about Church order was not about the ordination of women, but pointed out that Church order itself has been open to change and development throughout the history of the Church. Maybe it was the inference that mattered. Or perhaps the rector was worried about his own position. Who knows?

After dealing with the initial jolt of the cancellation, I was more amused than outraged to note that at age 82 I could still pose a threat! However, the fact that women could so easily be dismissed with no recourse was another example of the deep-rooted patriarchy that prevails in the Church.

Detroit—once a forward-looking archdiocese, is now, for the most part, more conservative and conformist. Yet, at the same time, people of a more radical bent and committed to justice on many fronts exercise their commitment in groups such as Pax Christi Michigan. Several "house churches" meet at regular intervals; there, lay people who often feel discouraged gather to celebrate the liturgy and share their faith.

Within the archdiocese, a group of priests and lay people have joined together in a support group called Elephants in the Living Room. The purpose of the group is to seek renewal of the Church in Detroit. Its website explains, "We do this by offering opportunities for education and creating an open forum for discussion and dialogue that will lead to developing and advocating more collegial solutions to the challenges we face. We firmly believe these efforts will contribute to a greater solidarity among priests and a renewed Church of Detroit."

Though somewhat controversial, especially with regard to the topics it discusses, the group is allowed to function freely, maintain its own website and publish its own documents. To me, this a positive sign from Cardinal Maida, even if the group is only tolerated within an archdiocese that is not publicly committed to discussion of the controversial issues. Rather than being "liberal" topics, these issues symbolize the values and need for communion, participation and Eucharist—that is, breaking the bread of life together.

The Archdiocese of Detroit is home to Bishop Thomas Gumbleton. Controversy has swirled around him not only because of his long commitment to peace and justice, but, more recently, and in particular, because of his address to the Ohio House Judiciary Committee on January 11, 2006, on behalf of those who were sexually abused by clergy. The bishop first apologized to the victims of clerical abuse. He stood behind those who argued for an extension of the statutes of limitation in order to provide an opportunity for the victims to have their day in court. But deeply embedded in his argument, and most especially, was the question of accountability involving not only the priest perpetrators, but the bishops who appeared to protect them. Without such full accountability, Bishop Gumbleton felt that the credibility of Church leaders as moral guides would be compromised. His intercession, his argument and intention, as one can imagine, were not welcomed or appreciated by the Ohio bishops. One suspects that the matter was referred to higher authority.

No longer allowed to live in the inner-city parish where he was pastor for more than a decade, Bishop Gumbleton, further, must now obtain the permission of any bishop in whose diocese he is asked to speak. This permission has sometimes been withheld, even if the invitation, as in one instance, was to give a retreat to a group of women religious.

Bishop Gumbleton, a great admirer of martyred Archbishop Oscar Romero of El Salvador, has made several trips to that country. His visits show solidarity with the Salvadoran people and raise Americans' consciousness about our nation's involvement in the repressive days of the civil war there and, even now, through free trade and immigration.

I have a sense that, like Romero, Bishop Gumbleton has "crossed a line" in the face of injustice and made a total commitment to the Gospel in spite of the consequences, including the very real risk of being misunderstood and misinterpreted.

He spends much of his time in peace-making endeavours both at home and abroad, and has an ever-lengthening list of awards, honorary degrees, and seemingly never-ending invitations to speak to groups on peace, justice, and a Church that places an emphasis there.

The archdiocese used to be home to Bishop Ken Untener, bishop of the Diocese of Saginaw, Michigan, who died in 2003 at the age of 66. Many IHM sisters served in a variety of ministries under the leadership of this very creative, practical theologian and prophet in and for the Church who, incidentally, has a sister in the IHM community. Those of us who were privileged to attend his consecration as bishop in November 1980 will never forget his words to the assembled congregation, words that he lived out with great simplicity: "Hi, I'm Ken. I'm here to be your waiter." The pastoral writings of Bishop Untener, entitled *The Practical Prophet,* offer a rich view of the breadth of his thought. In the epilogue to the book, his friend Archbishop John R. Quinn concluded with these words:

> Surely those who may find fault with one or other position taken in this book will feel challenged to emulate the charity and goodness of heart, the faith and perseverance of a humble Bishop who never forgot that he was a disciple.[16]

After Bishop Untener's death, the succeeding bishop reversed much of Ken's way of proceeding, and even suggested that his mandate and intention was "to clean up the diocese."

On January 28, 2009, Allen H. Vigneron was installed as the Archbishop of Detroit at the Cathedral of the Most Blessed Sacrament. A letter expressing his hopes as the Shepherd of this Archdiocese was on the first page of the program prepared for the installation:

> ... I ask you to join with me in praying that I will always be faithful to the commitments that I make today ... Let

us ask the Lord that He will give us the graces we need to respond to the tough times that we are experiencing along with our neighbors ... That He will guide us to a better future ... for wisdom to find solutions for building a better tomorrow.

2

The IHM Congregation: "The Blue Nuns Go Green"

The IHM Sisters have served Detroit since the congregations' beginnings in 1845. Today, that presence has been severely curtailed, not only through the closure of many parochial elementary and high schools, but even more seriously because of our diminishing numbers. Nevertheless, at its two most recent chapters (2001, 2005–06) the congregation not only restated and reaffirmed its commitment to the city, but also took on a deeper responsibility for the whole earth community.

While dedication to education is still at the heart of who we are as IHMs, its expression today is in areas that do not tend to be associated primarily with schools and colleges. The underlying direction of the congregation stated at chapter 2001 expresses well a new and expanded meaning of who we are as we respond to the cries of our times.

> We believe that everything before us brought us to this moment and we claim our future directions within the richness of our tradition. Impelled by the growing realization that we are interconnected with the whole

> web of life, and that the escalation of violence, increasing global poverty, and the exploitation of the earth threaten all of creation, we renew our passion to live the liberating mission of Jesus in the spirit of humility, simplicity and zeal. We choose to enflesh this call by working with others to build a culture of peace and right relationship among ourselves, with the Church and with the whole earth community.

That profoundly beautiful and underlying direction was reaffirmed once again at the chapter of 2005–06, where we renamed our commitment to build a culture of sustainability based in right relationships, economic and social justice, inclusivity and non-violence. One of the ways we as IHM sisters are trying to live out this pledge is by integrating the universe story, the Christian story, the earth story, the IHM story, and the Church story. That is a tall order, especially when we find ourselves in many places on the storyline!

The universe story has made us aware that a new world view challenges us and the way we express our faith as well. We are called to ongoing study, reflection and rearticulation of our deepest beliefs in ways that augment rather than contradict this new reality.

This grand and glorious vision is not easily implemented. It presents a major challenge not only to the leadership of the congregation, but also to each of us who hold and live the Catholic faith. How to integrate these stories in a practical way is daunting. Even more important is determining the kind of study and theological reflection that will make such integration possible. It will require more than a superficial reading of articles, watching of videos, taking congregational stands, or engaging with the insights of scientists and theologians. How will it become a way of life? How will we find the deepest expression of our Catholic faith, our commitment to the Gospel and to the mission of Jesus in the reality of these times in light of a deeper understanding of our planet and indeed of the whole cosmos? How do these realities influence the stands we take, the positions we support and the spirituality we profess? Moreover, how will these aspects of faith light up and challenge those with whom we minister and interact?

I often feel that I lag far behind what I am called to be. Working for the sustainability of the planet is an overwhelming task, given the violent and greedy tendencies of our world and culture. How can I translate the loftiness and beauty of our chapter commitment into the nitty-gritty of everyday life? How can I remain on the lofty plain of such idealism yet make practical decisions that support those ideals? I encounter these questions every day. Above all, I need and long for a more constant call and challenge to live this out from and in the Church, whose life is to nourish and give meaning to our own lives, but often fails to do so. Many women religious today (like countless others who share our faith) feel alienated from the Church. I look with hope and expectation to our congregational leaders and pray that they will continue to call and encourage us.

In January 2007, Mary Ellen Sheehan, IHM, at the request of the IHM Leadership Council, published a working paper entitled "Four Stories: Integrating the Universe Story, the Christian Story, the Earth Story and the IHM Story" to help us understand the challenges of today. The opening introductory paragraph articulates the purpose:

> Reflecting on the interrelationship of the scientific story of the universe, the Christian narrative, the Earth story today, and our IHM story is challenging and stimulating. These four stories are unique, and each one is amazing. We live in them in an all-at-once way, and while they have different time spans, they are equally important to us. They describe our context; they give us images, symbols, and truths that shape our values. They reveal our life's call and purpose, individually and in community;

they source our cultivating God's life in us and circling
it about widely in our world today.

Her clear and articulate presentation will, it is hoped, be a catalyst not only for our congregation but also for all those who seek to integrate this new world view in their lives.

At home in Monroe, we chose a sustainable design and construction when we renovated the mother house. The renovation has earned a number of prestigious awards. This work is a testimony to our convictions about right relationships with the earth. It is also a call and challenge for those of us who live or will live in the mother house in the future: as women religious, our greatest message to all is that God and all creation are at the heart of this community.

3

The Gift and Grace of Fewness

The renovations to the mother house resulted in a sizeable debt. Perhaps this risk seems reckless, irresponsible, in this moment of great change. At the same time, it pledges us to the future. It says that we trust that our ideals will continue and bear fruit in ways that are not yet clear to us. How we claim our lives as apostolic women involves accepting that as the years go by, our numbers will become fewer. As I reflected on this point, I came across a poem from *The Thomas Merton Poems* by J.S. Porter, a Canadian poet whose reflections on fewness offered some inspiration as well as a framework for my own thoughts.

> There's too much of everything
> books, stars, flowers.
> How can one flower be precious
> in a bed of thousands?
> How can one book count
> in a library of millions? …
> Yet something remains
> the dream of fewness
> one woman, one man.[17]

Perhaps the dream of fewness seems to send the wrong message as we reimagine and reconfigure our lives as a group. And yet, the reimagining and reconfiguring offer a way of drawing fewness into a new design.

Our inevitable circling back to fewness is both gift and grace: an opportunity to claim once again the origins and mission of our beginnings—our basic identity—when we were more ecclesial than ecclesiastical. It was only a little more than a century ago that as communities with simple vows we were officially acknowledged to be religious in the canonical sense. Perhaps it is time to re-embrace our humble origins, which linked us more closely to our lay sisters and brothers than to the official Church.

No longer the Church's corps of professionals, we can be less elitist and more present among the laity, who should be the principal bearers of evangelization. We already see the fruits of this shift in focus as we broaden our membership to include lay associates and others who share our goals. We work for the greater good when we use our gifts in theological reflection and social analysis to enable all lay women to claim their own power in patriarchal structures.

The prophetic charism at the heart of religious life is that we are not called to *do* something but to *be* something—to be witnesses to the primacy of God and to the union with God that is the destiny of all people, and to communicate, through solidarity with the poor and abandoned, the message that God loves them so very dearly in their poverty. That great good news is the essence of the Gospel and the challenge of Jesus, to whom we have committed ourselves. Religious life today is not a relic of an age that is past, but a compelling, ongoing, evolving way of living the Gospel.

The power of religious orders in building up the Church through schools, hospitals and social agencies has been an incredible gift that offers testimony to their care for others. Yet it has always been our deepest hope that such ministries witnessed above all to the mission of Jesus that incarnates God's love and

God's presence, compassion and care, for and to each person. This view has led us in recent decades to move into wider circles of care and to challenge various structures of our society, particularly those that cause so much suffering and injustice: racism, sexism, poverty and violence. In a future characterized by fewness rather than by numbers and organizational power, we can be more attentive to the victims of these unjust structures, even as we challenge the powerful to change them.

In countries throughout the world, millions suffer from violence, disease, hunger and malnutrition. Theologian Gustavo Gutierrez has asked, "How do you say to the poor, to the oppressed, to the insignificant, 'God loves you,' when their suffering seems to be the result of the negation and failure of love?" This is a question that plagues me as well. Our best answer is to continue to work for the eradication of unjust structures and, above all else, to enable the poor (and ourselves as well) to contemplate the mystery of death and resurrection as it is lived every day.

Gutierrez notes that, in the last analysis, the real question of the book of Job is this: "Can you love God for nothing?"

As I "see again" all the changes in religious life that I have lived through, and try to "see anew" its present reality, I turn to the reflections of two women religious who have written so well and with such challenge on this way of life.

More than a decade ago, Joan Chittister wrote *The Fire in These Ashes*, the title of which is her symbol for the future of religious life. The Gaelic practice of *Grieshog* involves burying warm coals in ashes at night in order to preserve the fire for the cold morning to come. The old fire is not allowed to die; it keeps its heat under heaps of ash through the long, dark night so that it can leap to life again at first light.

Sandra Schneiders's two volumes on religious life, in the series "Religious Life in the New Millennium," with a third volume on the way, find meaning in the metaphor of the treasure in the field: it is worth selling all to possess this field and the treasure it contains.

For both Chittister and Schneider, religious life is primarily a call to reclaim a way of life that has been organized to pursue the human quest for God. To keep the question of God—and God's questions—high on the horizon of the world is worth the gift of our lives. The proper question for religious life is not "What shall it become?" but "What is it now?" How we answer will make all the difference. As I ponder this last question—"What is religious life *now?*"—I am conscious that its answer will be partly framed by us as we respond to the decree of the Vatican's Congregation for Institutes of Consecrated Life and Societies of Apostolic Life to undertake an Apostolic Visitation of institutes of women religious in the United States. This decree, issued on December 22, 2008, reached us during the winter of 2009.

Not long ago, all of us IHM octogenarians who are still "out on mission" received a letter from the leadership council asking about our retirement plans. We were reminded that there are rooms for us ... a place at "home."

In 1945, the centennial of the IHM congregation and the year I entered the community, Sister Rosalita Kelly, IHM, published an official history of the IHM congregation entitled *No Greater Service.* A companion volume recounts the stories of our "missions"—the schools to which we were sent—and of IHM life in the convents. The Monroe IHMs have always called their mother house "home." It was not only where we were formed. It was also where, for many years, all IHM sisters who were not away studying came in the summer months to take refresher courses, finish first degrees, renew friendships, and make their annual retreat. And then, as Sister Rosalita poignantly (and a bit romantically) writes, "when diminishing physical powers give warning that the journey's end is not far distant, Home welcomes them as tired veterans ... cares for their bodies and souls with a charity so lovely as to make Christ's promise of the hundredfold almost an understatement."

Well, here I am, surely a veteran, not really very tried nor tired, and not sure at all that I welcome the invitation to "go home." What I will do in these latter years is far from clear to me. But I hope that they will be fruitful and meaningful, an offering for this Church, even if only in hope and longing.

At this time of my life, I am reminded of a quote from the *Diary of Virginia Woolf*:

> I can only note that the past is beautiful because one never realizes an emotion at the time. It expands later, and thus we don't have complete emotions about the present, only about the past … That is why we dwell on the past, I think.[18]

I reflect on what is there for me now in the Church, in religious life, and in my own self. My emotions and reflections about current events and experiences are only half formed, and I am less clear about their meaning. In years to come, if such years are given to me, I will likely look back at them with more perspective.

The prophetess Anna was 84 when "she spoke of the child to all who looked forward to the deliverance of Jerusalem." Perhaps that is the challenge for the octogenarians among us: to serve God day and night through prayer and to proclaim a message of hope and deliverance from the bondage of our world—and yes, even from some restrictive aspects in the Church of our own time.

Epilogue

My life has been a long love affair with the Church, beginning, I think, in the fourth grade when I received my first St. Andrew Daily Missal. As I learned to move the coloured ribbons back and forth between the Ordinary of the Mass, the appropriate preface, the readings of the day and the Feasts of the Saints, I saw that what I was doing was not unlike what the priest at the altar was doing with the big red book that lay on its golden stand covered with the appropriate liturgical colour.

Like all love affairs, mine has had its seasons. Writing these memoirs has served to highlight that journey—the initial budding of life, the high noon of summer, the rich harvest of autumn, and the wintry blasts of penetrating cold. Each season has its own beauty, its own colour.

In my Farmington Hills home, I have a place of study. This is my monastery. Here, the books that meant the most to me in my teaching years at Regis surround me with warmth and memories. It is from this little monastery that I do some writing, reflecting and remembering. On the wall to my left, next to the desk, are two framed items. Both express in symbolic ways what is unresolved and unfinished in me, in my hopes and desires, my thoughts and feelings.

One is a copy of a painting called "The Wounded Angel" by Hugh Simberg, a Finnish symbolist painter. It depicts two young peasant boys carrying a wounded angel on a stretcher. Her eyes are covered with a bandage; she cannot see. We do not know the source of the wound. One boy looks straight ahead. The other, who confronts us with a very direct gaze, seems to question the viewer. Some interpreters see the angel as the Church being carried out of the "city" to be tended in the "countryside" by the simple and poor of the world.

The other item is a copy of Gerard Manley Hopkins's "Spring and Fall: To a Young Child"—a facsimile of the poem written in his own hand and dated September 1880. It is a kind of first draft that includes some corrections. He is addressing a young girl named Margaret, who is weeping over the trees that have lost their leaves in the fall weather.

Margaret, are you grieving
Over Goldengrove unleaving?
Leaves, like the things of man, you
With your fresh thoughts care for, can you?
Ah! as the heart grows older,
It will come to such sights colder
By and by, nor spare a sigh
Where worlds of wanwood leafmeal lie.
Now no matter, child, the name:
Sorrow's springs are the same.
Nor mouth had, no nor mind, expressed
But heart heard of, ghost guessed:
It is the blight man was born for,
It is Margaret you mourn for.

Both of these works of art may seem sombre, but, for me, they are quite the opposite.

"The Wounded Angel" is a picture of hope for the healing of the Church, not by the hierarchy alone, nor only through structural changes, but by simple good people in the countryside, on the margins, or in the middle—by the people of God, the whole of us, to whom the wounded Church has been entrusted and in whom it lives.

Hopkins's poem initially attracted me because of young Margaret in the spring of life to whom the question is asked, and Margaret in the fall of her years to whom the answer is given. In the spring of life, it takes no effort or reflection to name the immediacy of our sorrow. It is sharp and tangible, but often it is deceptive as well. In the fall years, however, after many seasons of lived experience, we are able to name that deepest sorrow from inner springs: false expectations and unrealistic dreams. "It is Margaret you grieve for." The poem is a reminder to claim yet again— over and over—"the one thing necessary."

At the Jesuit spirituality centre in Guelph, Ontario, a rock garden is built into the right angle formed by the wall of the chapel and the large common room of the retreat house. A beautiful vista of rolling land extends beyond it. In the rock garden is a statue of St. Ignatius. He is bent forward, his cloak billowing behind him, walking into the wind—a man on a mission. A couple of winters ago, during a very cold February, I made a retreat at Guelph. Each day, I spent some time looking out the floor-to-ceiling common room windows at the stark beauty formed by ice and snow.

One day, I noticed something I had not "seen" before—a large piece of driftwood that seemed to be cemented to the wall of the chapel. A closer look revealed the features of an old woman enfolded in a hooded cloak. She is seasoned; the wind does not shake her. She is not carved from the wood; rather, the wood has shaped her. There she stands like a sentinel in the snow, long icicles hanging menacingly over her head from the overhang of the roof. Like St. Ignatius, she looks out across the garden to the east, but she is not in motion. What a jolt she gave me! Is she

Anna, the prophetess? And then the old woman shocked me into a new recognition. Is she me? An octogenarian standing glued to the wall of the Church awaiting and hoping for the promise of things yet to come? Was the Church holding me up in some unseen way? Was I holding up the Church?